WORTHY

Navigating Setbacks & Life's Messy Middles

A guide to cultivating self-worth

Dr. Kasmin Boswell

Copyright © 2025 Kasmin Boswell

All rights reserved. No part of this book may be used or reproduced in any manner whatsoever without written permission except in the case of brief quotations embodied in critical articles or reviews.

Thank you for buying an authorized edition of this book and for complying with copyright laws by not reproducing, scanning, or distributing any part of it in any form without permission. You are supporting writers and their hard work by doing this.

Published in the United States of America

First Edition, 2025.

ISBN: 979-8-9995615-0-3

Disclaimer

This book is intended for informational and inspirational purposes only. It is not a substitute for professional advice, diagnosis, or treatment. Readers should seek the advice of qualified professionals regarding any physical, mental, or emotional health concerns. The author and publisher disclaim any liability arising directly or indirectly from the use or application of the information contained in this book.

Some names, identifying details, and certain events may have been changed to protect the privacy of individuals. Any resemblance to actual persons, living or dead, is purely coincidental.

*"When we deny our stories,
they define us.
When we own our stories,
we get to write the ending."*

— *Brené Brown, Rising Strong (2015)*

DEDICATION

To my mother, *"Queen"* Ann Boswell–you taught my brother and me to love each other unconditionally, unapologetically; to let our goodness of character, compassion, and integrity be the sweet fragrance we leave with every soul we encounter.

To Waraire, Stephen Ford, Imelda Trejo, Ian Alexander Jr., Mrs. Bev–gone far too soon, yet never will you be forgotten. To Uncle Walter and my nephews, Miles, and Mason–each of you reminds me daily what it means to show up authentically and always *"check my mentals"* so the world gets the most phenomenal version of me.

It has been a great experience to be loved by such genuinely caring souls. Know that I love you to the moon and back, forevermore.

ENDORSEMENTS

"Kasmin serves up a bounty of food for thought, along with a practical plan of action to help you become your personal best. Yes, you can be renewed by the changing of your mind—and this book proves it!"
— **CINDY HERRON-BRAGGS,** *Grammy-nominated singer, actress, model, and founding member of En Vogue*

"I was lucky enough to meet Kasmin in 1997, when she was a rising star and participant in CLASS. Since then, I've watched her grow into a swan, gracefully bringing forth her wisdom. We're blessed that she now chooses to share her insights with us. It's been an honor to mentor Kasmin throughout her journey toward self-worth. Walking in the footsteps of her time with Florence Littauer, she offers this book as a guide to valuing oneself. Unlike many how-to books, this one invites you on a journey not only to follow in the author's footsteps, but also to engage with tangible concepts and practical exercises along the way."

— **LAUREN LITTAUER BRIGGS,** *CLASS Trainer, Author: The Art of Helping—What to Say and Do When Someone is Hurting; Making the Blue Plate Special—The Joy of Family Legacies. Co-founder of www.livingyourbestlife60plus.com; www.LaurenBriggs.com*

"Worthy is more than a book—it's a lifeline for anyone who's ever found themselves stuck in the messy middle of life, questioning their value, their choices, and their strength to carry on. Kasmin opens her heart with raw honesty and grace, sharing her journey through loss, betrayal, and the crushing weight of perfectionism, yet she never gave up on herself. Her book is a beautiful testament to resilience, healing, and the quiet power within when everything else falls apart. I'm proud to call her my friend and even prouder to witness the light she continues to bring into the world."
— **DOROTHY NEWTON,** *Author, Speaker, Co-Host Daystar Joni Table Talk*

"While American church culture drifts the unconscious sea of wretchedness, Worthy: Navigating the Messy Middles, throws us a lifeline. Requiring only the riddance of any ingrained worthlessness, this timely work offers in return a new worship praxis flowing from our worth-ship. Join Dr. Kasmin Boswell on the journey of reclaiming your innate worth and internal wealth. This book will leave you not only reflecting more deeply, but walking more freely, anchored in truth and empowered by grace."
— **D.E. PAULK,** *Author of The Holy Bible of Inclusion, M.T.S. Global Religions, Emory University*

"We all live in an ever-changing world, burdened by extreme demands on our consciousness and unrealistic expectations, both external and internal. This book serves as a much-needed reset, helping you reconnect with your greatest asset: yourself. It emphasizes your internal happiness, rather than the expectations of others. As I journeyed through its pages as a dedicated professional, it helped me refocus on what truly matters: to disengage from

Endorsements

superficial distractions and identify the energy drains that can leave you so depleted, you no longer recognize yourself."

— **DR. NAPOLEON HIGGINS Jr.**, *Child, Adolescent & Adult Psychiatrist; Executive Director of the Black Psychiatrists of America, Past President of the Caucus of Black Psychiatrists of America Psychiatric Association, NEI (Neuroscience Education Institute) Congress Faculty*

"As a trial lawyer who has spent decades fighting for justice in courtrooms and communities, I know firsthand how easy it is to overlook your worth when the world keeps telling you otherwise. Worthy: Navigating Life's Messy Middles is the kind of book that stops you in your tracks—and reminds you that your story isn't over just because it's gotten hard. It's a powerful reminder that your story doesn't end in the struggle—it begins there. As someone who's spent my career fighting for people overlooked, attacked, and underestimated, I recognize the truth in Dr. Kasmin Boswell's words. She doesn't sugarcoat the process of rebuilding; she lays it out with honesty, insight, and grit. This book speaks to anyone navigating loss, fear, or change—and gives them the tools to rise stronger, with dignity intact.

— **MICHAEL L. WRIGHT, ESQ.**, *Trial Attorney, Advocate for Justice, Member, Multi-Million Dollar Advocates Forum / Partner, Wright & Schulte, LLC*

"Just like the game of football, understanding your worth doesn't happen when it's easy—it happens in the messy middle, when everything's on the line. Dr. Kasmin Boswell's book reminds us that growth isn't clean or comfortable, but it is necessary. I encourage you to complete the exercises. Put in the work. Because real strength—on the field or in life—comes from knowing who you are when the play breaks down and you've got to dig deep. This book will help you do just that."

— **KELLEN WINSLOW SR.**, *Pro Football Hall of Fame, Class of 1995*

"Honey, let me tell you—life will body-slam you, throw you into the turnbuckles, and then have the nerve to ask why your hair's messed up. "Dr. Kasmin Boswell gets it. This book? Oh, this book is like that homegirl who grabs you by the shoulders, looks you dead in the eye, and says, 'Mija... you are WORTHY.' And not when life is all cute and filtered either—but right in the messy middle, when you're holding it together with duct tape, prayers, and cafecito. I laughed, I cried, I cussed... and then I got my life together. Read the book. Do the exercises. Trust me. Because surviving ain't enough—it's time to thrive, baby."

— **TANYA RUSSELL (Cha Cha Sandoval-McMahon)**, *Comedy Pioneer & Hollywood's First Minority Stuntwoman*

"Reading Worthy felt like a heart-to-heart with my inner self. It's the kind of book that reminds you to embrace every part of your journey, even the messy middles. Just like designing a swimwear line, understanding your worth requires creativity, resilience, and a touch of fun. Dr. Boswell beautifully captures this essence, encouraging us to celebrate our uniqueness and navigate life's challenges with grace and confidence."

— **VY NGUYEN**, *Founder & CEO of Paradise Club and Lolli Swim*

"I met Dr. Kasmin Boswell during our doctoral program and was immediately struck by her rare combination of intellectual brilliance and deep spiritual wisdom. Worthy reflects exactly that: a beautiful, practical guide for navigating life's transitions, filled with insight, compassion, and a reminder that the answers we seek are always within."

— **DR. JOY L. SALVETTI**, *Faculty Emeritus, California State University, Sacramento; Author; Poet*

Endorsements

"As those of us in medicine know, healing often unfolds in quiet, uncertain places we don't immediately see—the messy middles. In Worthy, Dr. Kasmin Boswell brings that truth into sharp, empowering focus. A compassionate guide and gifted teacher, Kasmin offers insights and practical exercises that help us tap into our inner resilience—no different than nurturing a patient's quiet strength through chronic illness or recovery. Whether you're navigating change, grief, or self-doubt, this book meets you exactly where you are and helps you discover that you are enough—and worthy—right now."

— **RAFFI TACHDJIAN,** *MD, MPH, Assistant Clinical Professor of Medicine & Pediatrics, UCLA Division of Allergy & Clinical Immunology; Founder, Children's Music Fund*

"Worthy is a gentle but powerful reminder that we are not our pain—we are our ability to grow through it. Dr. Boswell offers a compassionate roadmap for healing, especially for those who've ever felt unseen."

— **VARTAN TACHDJIAN,** *MD, Pediatrician, Homeless Advocate, Author: Return to Homelessness*

"As a pioneer in TMS and longtime advocate for advancing mental health care, I've worked alongside many gifted minds—but few with Dr. Boswell's precision, heart, and tenacity. In Worthy, she brings the same clarity and compassion she used to help patients gain access to care. It's a thoughtful, deeply human guide to navigating life's most uncertain chapters."

— **SAAD A. SHAKIR,** *MD, DLFAPA, Retired Stanford Faculty; Founder, Silicon Valley TMS*

AUTHOR'S NOTE

Have you ever faced setback after setback, until not even sleep offers any solace? Have you spent so much time being there for others that you've left no space for yourself, unable to meet your own needs?

I know that feeling all too well.

At one point in my life, I experienced a diminished sense of worth—as if the universe was screaming that everyone else mattered more than me. I couldn't figure out why, even though I showed up for countless others, no one ever felt compelled to save me. And the few who did often judged, lost interest, or simply walked away.

I went through an unwanted yet necessary divorce, workplace harassment, bullying, and betrayal by family, friends, and associates. On top of that, I lost my brother, business partner, friend, and someone I viewed as a son—far too soon—to cancer.

Worthy

All I kept thinking was, *"How and why could this happen to me?"* I stayed in school and got the doctorate. My brother Waraire and I scored a deal to create uniforms for McDonald's, and dress LeBron James, Jay-Z, Stevie Wonder, Aldis Hodge, Raphael Saadiq, countless NBA athletes, as well as Hollywood agents. We collaborate with Mitchell & Ness and earn regular praise in GQ, Esquire, and The Hollywood Reporter. My brother even worked for Will Smith and Wesley Snipes, for crying out loud!

But when life unraveled, I people-pleased, dug deeper, and gave more—without realizing that in doing so, I was sacrificing my joy, boundaries, peace, finances, strength, and time.

I had been my own worst enemy, trapped in a cycle of self-blame and unrealistic expectations. I thought my messy middle couldn't get any worse, until it became a dumpster fire that consumed everything I had left.

Then one day, as I sat at home listening to Bob Marley's Redemption Song, something clicked. The lyrics spoke of breaking free from mental chains and, in that moment, I realized it wasn't the universe punishing me. I was the one holding myself back.

Nothing I went through was my fault. Things happen. What mattered was how I responded. I had spent too long living in a negative mindset, believing I was unworthy. It was time to rewrite my story.

And that's what this book is about.

In it, you will learn how to show up and meaningfully respond, rather than merely act and react. You'll discover how to reframe setbacks into valuable lessons and reclaim your sense of self.

Life is unpredictable. There will be hardships, losses, and pain. But how you handle them defines your path forward.

Join me in becoming "excuse-less" and "unrealistic" about what life has in store for YOU.

INTRODUCTION

Worthy—a word that has been twisted and misconstrued over time.

How often have you questioned your worth? Maybe it was when you didn't land the job, when your achievements went unnoticed, or when you felt like no matter how much you did, it was never enough. Society teaches us that worth is something we earn—measured by our successes, our possessions, or the approval of others. But that's a misconception we've been taught.

Worth isn't a number, a title, or external validation. It is something inherent, something that has been yours since the moment you came into being. More importantly, it doesn't come from the loud voices of the crowd but from the quiet voice within.

Now more than ever, we need to recalibrate our understanding of worth. In a world where social media subtly shapes how we see ourselves, it's easy to get lost in the comparisons and curated feeds. But the problem runs deeper. Beyond the endless scroll, what else is eroding our sense of self-worth? Why does this decline feel so pervasive?

In my experience, the decline in self-worth that so many people are experiencing today is deeply tied to a mix of modern societal pressures that chip away at our self-esteem. And if I'm being honest, one of the biggest culprits is our culture of perfectionism, which has a tight grip on everything from work to school. We've gotten to the point where every little thing can be rated, and we don't realize how those tiny five stars can mess with someone's head in the worst possible way. The thing is, it's not just others we're holding to these impossible standards—we do it to ourselves, too.

We've become so obsessed with achievement and productivity that we've forgotten what it means to take care of ourselves. The pressure to meet these ridiculously high expectations—ones that, let's face it, no one can meet all the time—leaves us feeling inadequate. And when I say *"ridiculously high,"* I mean it. No one can be performing at 100% all the time. It's just not human. But here's the thing: the endless chase for perfection doesn't just leave us mentally exhausted and emotionally drained. It also makes it harder to recognize and appreciate what makes us truly unique.

Of course, our obsession with perfection is also rooted in something bigger: economic instability and job insecurity. We're all working harder than ever just to make what we used to. Even if your paycheck has grown a bit, you still probably feel like you're not getting ahead, thanks to inflation. In a world where so much of our value is tied to what we earn or how well we're doing at work, anyone struggling financially or dealing with unemployment can start to feel like they're worth less as a person. The gig economy and temporary jobs only make this worse, leaving people in a state of constant stress and anxiety, which takes a toll on their sense of self-worth.

Introduction

But the truth is, the roots of this constant striving go much deeper. For many of us, it starts back in childhood, where overachieving and perfectionism were the expectations. The drive to *"perform"* for love—the idea that our worth was tied to what we could accomplish—shaped how we saw ourselves in some pretty profound ways. And as we've gotten older, that pressure has only grown.

From a young age, kids today are facing crushing educational pressures. High-stakes testing, endless grading, and the race to get into the best schools all teach them that their value is tied to academic success. This early lesson in competition doesn't just impact their performance—it can take a serious toll on their self-esteem, especially for those who don't fit the traditional academic mold.

The bottom line is this: our sense of worth is being tugged in every direction, and it doesn't look like it's going to stop anytime soon. If we're ever going to embrace our messy middles—the parts of us that aren't perfect—we're going to need to figure out how to redefine what makes us truly worthy and start seeing it for what it really is.

What's in This Book?

I wrote this book because I want you to understand something: your real power comes from embracing your imperfections and learning to truly know yourself.

It's about showing up in the *"waiting rooms"* of life with patience, taking small but intentional steps toward a life that feels right for you. If this resonates, then keep reading—here's what you can expect in the chapters ahead:

1. **Redefining Worth:** I'm going to start by challenging what most people think about worth. We'll dive into a broader, more inclusive way of understanding your value that doesn't rely on the usual measures.

2. **Recognizing Your Worth:** This is where the magic happens. Through practical exercises and moments of reflection, I'll guide

you in recognizing your worth, especially when the world around you is determined to tell you otherwise.

3. **Common Human Desires:** We all have fundamental needs that make us feel valued—things like connection, respect, and love. I'll explore how we can meet these needs in healthy, fulfilling ways that truly affirm who we are.

4. **The Role of Character & Gifting:** Your talents, your character—they're not just *"nice qualities"*; they are the heart of your self-worth. Together, we'll look at how these elements shape your sense of value.

5. **Navigating Life's Challenges:** Life throws curveballs. From dealing with anxiety to managing inevitable changes, I'll help you find strategies to keep your sense of worth intact when life feels overwhelming.

The goal of this book is clear: to help you live a life where your worth is anchored in a deep, personal understanding and acceptance of who you are. But let me be clear: there's no quick fix. This book won't change everything overnight. Think of it as a starting point—a chance to shift how you see yourself and your place in the world. Your journey is about making peace with who you are right now while still dreaming of who you can become.

The truth here is simple, yet powerful: you are the one person you will spend your entire life with. As Ernest Hemingway wisely said in The Sun Also Rises (1926), *"You can't get away from yourself by moving from one place to another."* But when your sense of worth is secure, the external circumstances lose their grip on you.

To get there, we need to set aside everything we've been taught to value and start discovering what truly matters to us. After all, as Emily Dickinson so beautifully put it, *"I dwell in possibility"* (1890).

Let's take that to heart and explore the possibility of finding and fully embracing your true worth—a worth that lives in every present moment, in the 'nows' we create and cherish.

CONTENTS

Introduction xi
Chapter 1: Reclaiming Your Worth 1
    The Lure of Perfection 2
    The Influence of Social Media 8
    Focusing on the Process, Not the Metrics 11
Chapter 2: Seeing the Value Within 17
    Identifying Moments of Value 19
    The Challenge of External Judgments 25
    The Gift of Being Disadvantaged 28
Chapter 3: The Desires That Drive Us 33
    Values and Their Origins 34
    Influence of Resources 39
    Belief Systems and Worldviews 42

Chapter 4: Character and Gifts 45
    Natural Gifts and Their Impact.. 46
    Success and Setbacks Based on Character 48
    The Role of Introversion in Character Building........................ 52

Chapter 5: Ditch the Fear 59
    Understanding the Roots of Anxiety... 60
    Breaking the Cycle of Worry 71
    Overcoming Addictive Behaviors and Finding Peace............... 75

Chapter 6: Change is Power.. 79
    Navigating Life's Transitions.. 80
    The Power of Flexibility and Adaptability................................. 86
    Cultivating Resilience in Uncertainty 96

Chapter 7: Comparison Kills... 99
    The Trap of Constant Comparison 100
    Staying True to Your Values Amid External Pressures........... 105
    Building Integrity and Celebrating Your Unique Path 110

Chapter 8: Cutting Through the Noise 117
    Identifying and Minimizing Distractions 118
    The Impact of Technology on Focus and Self-Worth 120
    Practicing Mindfulness to Maintain Clarity............................... 126

Chapter 9: Strength in Support 135
    The Importance of Healthy Relationships 137
    Recognizing and Releasing Toxic Connections........................ 141
    Creating a Supportive Network for Growth 146

Chapter 10: True Wealth 153
    Shifting Perspectives on Financial Success 155
    The Connection Between Money and Self-Worth................... 163
    Creating Wealth That Aligns with Your Values....................... 165

Parting Words 171
Acknowledgments 175
About the Author 179
References and Citations 181

CHAPTER 1

RECLAIMING YOUR WORTH

"You are your best thing."
— *Toni Morrison*

Jane Fonda in Five Acts is a documentary directed by Grammy Award-winner Susan Lacy. But it's more than just a glimpse into Jane Fonda's life – it's like sitting down with her over coffee, listening to her share the highs and lows of her incredible journey. She's been in the spotlight since 1960, and through this intimate look, we see her wrestle with the weight of always trying to be perfect. It's clear that striving for an ideal, impossible to reach, has left its mark on her.

Lacy does something incredible here: she pulls back the curtain on the real, often unseen side of being a public figure. Jane opens up about her unrelenting pursuit of perfection, whether as an actress, an activist, or just as a woman trying to measure up. It's honest and raw. She tells us how chasing this ideal often left her feeling empty, never quite good enough. And in that, Jane drives home one of the most important lessons: perfectionism isn't just a barrier to happiness – it's toxic. (Lacy, 2018)

But what really stands out in this documentary is how Jane's story evolves into something much bigger. It's not just about Jane—it's a powerful commentary on the destructive nature of perfectionism itself. It reveals the pressure we all feel to fit into a mold that matches society's impossible standards. We magnify every little flaw, holding ourselves to an image that just isn't human. Our worth becomes tangled in an unattainable ideal that we can never reach.

Watching Jane's journey unfold, it's impossible not to reflect on our own lives. How often are we too hard on ourselves, constantly pushing to meet unrealistic expectations that don't even reflect who we truly are? When I watched this documentary, two questions kept echoing in my mind: Why do we hold onto these ideals? And what would it be like if we just let them go?

The Lure of Perfection

"If I can just redecorate my home…"

"If I can just get my PhD…"

"If I can just post the perfect vacation pictures…"

"…maybe they'll like me."

First off, who is 'they,' and why are you under the false assumption that they're any more 'perfect' than you are?

The truth is, no one has it all figured out. Billionaires end up in divorce court just as easily as someone on minimum wage. We all feel it—the pressure to have it together, to meet the ever-moving target of perfection. We chase this ideal as if it's the finish line of a race that promises happiness on the other side.

But here's the reality: perfection is a myth. Society paints this glossy picture of what life should look like – from magazine covers to social media feeds. We're constantly shown an image of perfection that feels not just attainable, but expected. What we often fail to see is that the pursuit of perfection isn't the key to happiness – it's a trap. It's an endless marathon, where the finish line just keeps moving farther and farther away.

Brené Brown really nails it in *The Gifts of Imperfection* (2010) . She speaks so powerfully about how chasing the illusion of 'perfect'—this ideal the world constantly pushes onto us—actually pulls us further away from our true selves. It's as if we're all running after this shiny, unattainable image, but the closer we get, the more we realize it's just a mirage. And in that chase, we find ourselves stuck in this perpetual state of striving – never truly able to just sit with ourselves and feel content with who we are, as we are.

And I mean content, not complacent.

Brené suggests something pretty radical, but also profoundly essential: embracing our vulnerabilities. Instead of tucking them away or pretending they don't exist, she invites us to see them as a source of strength. It's about showing up, being seen, and doing it all without your masks or the armor we so often hide behind in our relationships, careers, and even in our relationship with ourselves. That's where the real growth happens – not in chasing some polished standard someone else set for us.

What's truly game-changing about her approach is how it flips the whole concept of perfection on its head. It opens the door for us to recognize that our quirks, mistakes, and struggles aren't things to hide – they're part of what makes us uniquely us. And even more powerful, they connect us with others who are embracing their own imperfect journeys.

It's a breath of fresh air, especially in a world that often values appearance over authenticity. Brown invites us to break free from the relentless pressure of perfection and, instead, to find joy and self-worth in the real, messy, beautifully imperfect versions of ourselves.

The question is—how do we begin?

Exercise 1: Embracing Vulnerability

Let's take a moment to put Brené Brown's wisdom into practice. This exercise is all about leaning into your vulnerabilities, not as weaknesses, but as sources of power and connection. Grab a journal or a piece of paper, find a quiet space where you can be with yourself, and let's dive in.

Step 1: Self-Reflection

1.1. Identify Your Vulnerabilities

Think about the places in your life where you feel most vulnerable. These could be parts of who you are, experiences from your past, or even your fears about what the future holds. Write them down. Be honest with yourself here; this is a safe space just for you. No judgment.

<u>Example prompts:</u>

What situations make me feel exposed or insecure?

- Are there aspects of my past that I hold back from others, afraid of their judgment?

- What fears surface when I think about how others might see me?

1.2. Reflect on Your Feelings

For each vulnerability, take a moment to write a few sentences about how it makes you feel. Does it bring up fear, anxiety, or maybe even shame? Sit with those emotions. Acknowledge them, but don't judge them. Just notice.

Example prompts:

- How does this vulnerability make me feel in the moment?

- What thoughts come to mind when I think about this aspect of myself?

Step 2: Reframing Vulnerability

2.1. Find the Strength

Now, let's start turning things around. For each vulnerability you've identified, see if you can find a way to look at it as a strength. I know this might feel tough, but trust me—every vulnerability has a lesson in it. Every wound carries wisdom.

Example prompts:

- How has this vulnerability made me stronger or more resilient?

- In what ways does this vulnerability help me connect with others, or make me more empathetic?

2.2. Embrace the Power of Storytelling

Think about a time when you shared one of your vulnerabilities with someone else. How did it feel to open up? How did the other person react? More often than not, when we let ourselves be seen—raw and imperfect—it deepens our relationships and brings people closer.

Example prompts:

- Recall a positive experience where sharing a vulnerability led to a supportive response.

- How did sharing this part of yourself change your relationship with the other person?

Step 3: Taking Action

3.1. Practice Vulnerability in Small Steps

Choose one vulnerability from your list and make a plan to share it with someone you trust. This could be a friend, family member, or therapist. Start small and see how it feels to open up.

Example prompts:

- Who is one person I feel safe sharing this with?

- What's a small way I can start to express this vulnerability?

3.2. Create a Daily Affirmation

Repeat it to yourself daily as a reminder that embracing your true self, including your imperfect, vulnerable parts, is a powerful act of courage.

Example affirmation:

- "I am strong because I embrace my true self, including my vulnerabilities."

After you've shared your vulnerability and practiced your affirmation for a week, take some time to reflect. How did it feel? What shifts did you notice in yourself and others? Be gentle with yourself, and adjust as needed. This is a journey, not a destination, and each step forward is a step toward greater authenticity and connection.

Stepping into vulnerability is the first step toward embracing our imperfections as part of our authentic selves. There's something deeply beautiful about accepting that we are flawed—something empowering about saying, *"Here I am, mistakes and all. Love me or leave, because I choose to love myself."*

But let's be clear: being authentic is not the same as giving up or settling for less. It's not about dropping the ball on your goals, your self-care, or anything else you care about. It's about showing up and striving to be your best—**not** the best, but your **best**—in all that you do.

When we stop measuring ourselves against someone else's idea of perfection, we start to see our own worth. We begin to understand that our true selves are enough, exactly as we are.

The Influence of Social Media

One element of our lives that desperately needs our attention is social media—a tool that, for many, has become a funhouse mirror, distorting the way we see ourselves and others. The images we encounter are often highly curated snapshots of perfection, showcasing only the highs while erasing the lows. This constant stream of idealized moments can leave us feeling like we're somehow falling short, as if we're just not good enough. We forget that these images are edited, filtered, and constructed with intention, not the full, messy reality of life.

You know how it is when you scroll through your Insta feed and see someone's perfectly posed vacation photos, their glowing skin, their picture-perfect family life? For a moment, it can make you feel like you're doing it all wrong. It's like everyone else is living their best, flawless life while you are over here just trying to keep it together. But then, if you pause and think about it, you remember that those images are often just a snapshot of someone's highlight reel, not the whole, complicated picture.

It's so important to pause and really ask ourselves: What are we measuring when we turn to social media to define our worth? Is it the number of likes we get or the quality of the relationships we build? The truth is, social media platforms are designed to be addictive and crafted to keep us hooked. Every like, comment, and share is a tiny dose of validation, triggering a dopamine release–that feel-good neurotransmitter tied to pleasure and reward (Watson, 2024). But here's the catch: that instant gratification is fleeting and, over time, can pull us further away from the real, messy, beautiful connections that truly nourish us. It's a rush, really, much like the thrill we get from other addictive behaviors, such as gambling or even indulging in comfort foods. Our brain's reward system lights up, and just like that, we're hooked. Those likes and comments become our little fix, pushing us to chase after that same sense of validation, over and over again.

The problem is that this dopamine-fueled loop can be pretty dangerous. We end up in a cycle of constantly chasing external validation just to feel good about ourselves. And slowly, almost without realizing it, we start depending on those digital affirmations to keep our self-esteem afloat. Over time, this reliance can grow into a full-blown social media addiction, where our moods and sense of worth become inextricably tied to the feedback we get online. A post might rake in hundreds of likes today, but tomorrow it's buried under a fresh wave of content. And just like that, we're back at it, chasing that same fleeting validation. When the likes or comments don't come in as expected, we start to feel that familiar sting of inadequacy. We begin comparing ourselves to others, gazing at their carefully curated highlight reels , wondering why our lives don't measure up. It's a dangerous place to be, especially when we feel like we're constantly falling short.

When I first started using Instagram, posting snapshots of my day, it gave me a buzz to see all the likes and comments. Each reaction was almost a sign of approval that I'm cool, I'm popular, and I liked that feeling. The thing is, I found myself experiencing small tinges of disappointment when some of my posts got fewer reactions, making me wonder what was wrong with me. I know it sounds silly, but we all crave that approval and if social media gives us it, then we miss it when it's gone—call it the dopamine effect. Now that I've worked out how addictive it can be, I don't use social media anymore for external validation and, honestly? I feel free.

I do want to add that if you have ever felt this way, it's not your fault. Social media companies have carefully crafted these systems to be addictive, so you're not alone in feeling caught up in the cycle.

The fact that they have done so is no secret. Back in 2017, former Facebook executive Chamath Palihapitiya openly admitted that these platforms are designed to exploit psychological vulnerabilities and get users 'hooked' (Palihapitiya 2017). They do so by exploiting basic human psychology, using a variety of engineered design tools. Whenever it's a like, share, or comment, they know that you get a dopamine hit in your brain, which makes you crave more. As for scrolling, it's a way to get you to consume more content, keeping you engaged for much longer than you intended. As former Google design ethicist Tristan Harris has warned, the algorithms engineered into social media are there to maximize the time you spend on the platforms, with push notifications pulling you back to the app (Harris, 2019).

Although the initial aim of Facebook may have been to connect us, it turns out that most of these interactions are quite superficial. I often refer to it as 'unsocial media' because it can actually make us feel even more isolated. If you watched *The Social Dilemma* (2020), you'll recall how it exposed the way social media platforms use data-driven manipulation to keep people hooked. This isn't an accident. Social media is designed to make sure you stay on their platforms for as long as possible, driven by the desire to profit from your attention. No wonder it's so hard to resist.

Let's take a look at the bigger picture. It's not just about the instant gratification of likes and shares. This cycle is impacting our mental health in deeper ways. Research has shown that excessive social media use can increase feelings of depression and anxiety (Zubair, 2023). What's even more challenging is how these platforms can distort our sense of reality. We see these carefully curated snapshots of other people's lives, and it's easy to fall into the trap of believing that everyone else is living a better, more exciting life. It's a distortion that makes us feel less than, like we're somehow missing out or falling short.

Here's the hard truth: breaking free from this comparison game isn't simple, and it's not about just 'getting over it.' For so many of us, social media has become a lifeline, whether it's for business, staying connected with loved ones, or just keeping up with the world around us. But even with all the good that it can bring, we have to acknowledge that these online connections are often built on versions of ourselves that aren't the full picture. They're filtered, edited, and carefully crafted. Real, meaningful connection happens when we show up, authentically, offline; when we nurture the relationships that are grounded in reality.

It's a shift, a shift in focus from metrics and digital validation to meaningful, present connections. It might not be easy, but it's a step toward reconnecting with who we truly are, beyond the screen.

Focusing on the Process, Not the Metrics

Let's face it: we live in a world that loves measurable success. It's easier to count likes, followers, or the numbers on a paycheck than it is to measure the quieter, more personal growth happening inside us. But what if we shifted our focus—just a little bit—from the destination to the journey itself? What if we started celebrating the process, rather than just the prize?

This is about learning to find joy in the doing, not just the achieving. Let me bring you back to a thought I shared earlier: Emily Dickinson once said, *"Forever is composed of nows."* It's those everyday moments, the small steps forward, that weave together the fabric of our lives. Those moments matter; they are the places where real growth takes place.

At the end of the day, success isn't just about what you can show on paper or what others can see. It's about how you feel when you lay your head on the pillow at night. Did you do something today that made you feel alive? Did you show up as your true self? Did you act in alignment with your values?

I'm willing to wager that you've probably been so focused on what you *still* need to do that you haven't taken a moment to acknowledge how far you've actually come. It's so easy to miss the small wins, to overlook the present moment while chasing the next thing. But those little steps? They matter more than we give them credit for.

A lot of this comes from the fear of failure. But the thing is: the only real failure we experience is when we fail to see that mistakes, missteps, and setbacks aren't failures at all. In fact, they're an essential part of the journey toward success. Every time we stumble, we learn something valuable. Each challenge we face shapes us and strengthens our resilience.

When we fall down and get back up, we don't just pick ourselves up: we carry forward a deeper wisdom. And with that wisdom, we're able to move forward with more strength and clarity than we had before.

Many well-known figures have overcome great challenges in their lives and bounced back from extreme adversity. One of the most famous is Abraham Lincoln, a self-educated man who eventually became President of the United States. Not only did he struggle with depression after losing the love of his life to typhoid fever, but he also suffered from a rare genetic disorder called Marfan syndrome, which likely contributed to his unusually tall, thin frame, long limbs, and joint problems.

Apart from his personal struggles, including the loss of his young son, Lincoln faced several other setbacks throughout his life. His business failed, he went bankrupt, and he lost multiple elections. Yet, it's these events that seemed to fuel his determination. Let's not forget his leadership during the American Civil War and his commitment to abolishing slavery. The beliefs he held and actions he took exemplify extraordinary resilience in the face of adversity, making him a prime example of someone who got back on the horse after falling off several times.

It's the fear of failure that often holds us back from taking the risks that bring us closer to our dreams. We see it as something to avoid at all costs. But what if we stopped seeing failure that way? What if we could embrace it as part of our story, as a necessary chapter in our growth?

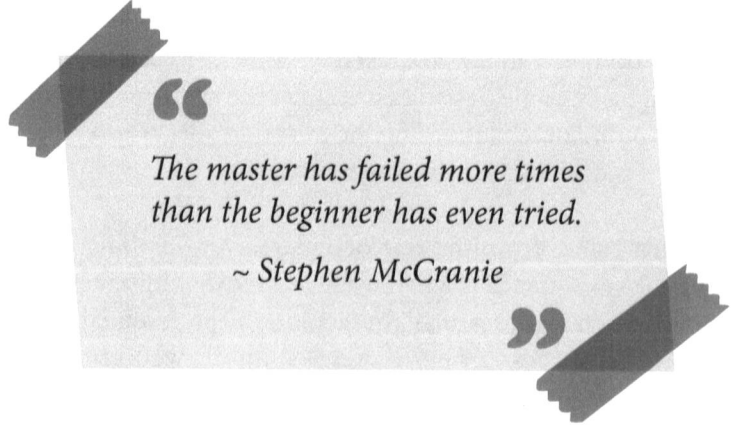

> *The master has failed more times than the beginner has even tried.*
>
> ~ Stephen McCranie

When we do face failure, it offers us a chance to pause and ask ourselves a tough question: Why did this happen? That *"why"* is so important—it's not just about what went wrong, but about understanding what it can teach us. This kind of reflection isn't only crucial for our personal and professional growth, it's vital for our spiritual growth too. So, we shouldn't run from it.

Yes, it can be uncomfortable. The initial sting of embarrassment can make us want to turn away. But once we move past that discomfort, we start to see things clearly. The *"why"* helps us pinpoint areas where we can improve, and that's where the magic happens. We can make changes, shift direction, and move forward with more wisdom.

Think about the countless entrepreneurs and innovators who have failed again and again. Many of them faced what seemed like impossible setbacks. But it was their resilience, their ability to bounce back after each failure, that gave them the strength to keep refining their ideas and pushing through. So many names come to mind: Thomas Edison, who famously said, *"I have not failed. I've just found 10,000 ways that won't work,"* after countless unsuccessful experiments to invent the light bulb; Henry Ford, who went from bankruptcy to revolutionizing the auto industry; and Walt Disney, who was fired from his first job for *"lacking imagination and having no good ideas."* Incredible, right?

If you haven't seen The Pursuit of Happyness (2006), starring Will Smith, I suggest you watch it. It portrays the true story of Chris Gardner, a struggling salesman who overcame severe hardships and even homelessness before becoming a multimillionaire. One of the most compelling scenes in the movie is when Chris finds himself sheltering in a subway station bathroom with his young son while someone is trying to kick the door in. His desire to protect his child in a moment of desperation reveals the raw sadness of his plight. But he never gives up and it's painful moments like this that make his success even more inspiring.

Here's the truth: failure is part of the process. It's not just a bump in the road—it's essential. It's through trial and error that we discover what works, what doesn't, and ultimately, how to create something meaningful.

This process isn't merely a stepping stone to success, it's the foundation of innovation and growth in every area of life.

Embracing failure is one of the keys to building resilience. Resilience is that quiet strength we carry inside us—the ability to rise, no matter how many times we fall. It's about being able to recover from setbacks, both big and small, and to keep moving forward. This resilience isn't only something that helps us in our careers; it's just as crucial in our relationships. Let's face it, misunderstandings, disagreements, and conflicts are a part of life. But how we respond to them—how we show up and stay open, even when things get messy—can truly shape our relationships and our lives.

If you see yourself picking up the pieces after a failure or a setback, you start to build a more balanced sense of self. Your worth doesn't depend on how others perceive you or on how *"silly"* you feel after a mistake. What matters is that you're still here, still trying, still learning. That's resilience.

Kristin Neff's work on self-compassion has been a game-changer in how we approach our own struggles. By learning to treat ourselves with kindness, we start to build a form of strength that doesn't rely on perfection. Self-compassion helps us replace that inner voice of self-criticism with a softer, more supportive tone. This shift doesn't only make life easier—it helps us face challenges with more confidence and less fear. (Neff, 2015)

Neff's research shows that people who practice self-compassion are more likely to bounce back from setbacks. They have higher emotional resilience and greater life satisfaction, as well as being less likely to experience anxiety or depression. This isn't about ignoring our flaws or pretending we don't make mistakes. It's about approaching ourselves and our struggles with understanding and patience. It's about being as gentle with ourselves as we would be with a loved one facing tough times.

So, the next time you catch yourself about to self-criticize or judge, pause for a moment. Take a deep breath and try something different: self-compassion. Treat yourself with the same kindness, patience, and understanding that you would offer a dear friend who's struggling. When you do approach yourself with compassion instead of criticism, you open the door to real growth. From this place of self-kindness, it becomes so much easier to escape the relentless grip of perfectionism.

Key takeaway:

There's a kind of freedom and relief that comes with embracing our imperfections—freedom that we often overlook while we're caught in the exhausting cycle of trying to fix ourselves. We believe that perfection is the goal, but what we don't realize is that this pursuit is not only unsustainable but also ultimately toxic. It steals our joy, our peace, and our sense of self-worth. Perfectionism can feel like an endless chase: there's always something more to do, something more to prove, and in that race, we lose sight of what truly matters: who we are right now, flaws and all.

The real liberation comes when we stop running from our imperfections. Instead of fearing or hiding our shadows, we can choose to embrace them. The parts of ourselves that we deem imperfect—those moments of failure, vulnerability, and discomfort—are exactly where our strength and growth lie. They are not things to be ashamed of; they are the threads that weave our humanity together. By accepting our flaws, we create space for authenticity, connection, and joy.

Let's stop aiming for perfection and start aiming for growth. Because the truth is, it's our imperfections that make us whole. They are not the opposite of success—they are the very things that help us become who we are meant to be.

CHAPTER 2

SEEING THE VALUE WITHIN

"The most common way people give up their power is by thinking they don't have any."
— Alice Walker

So, we have started recognizing our worth, learning how to nurture it, and how to stop outsourcing it to the opinions of others. But here's the real question: What actually makes us feel valuable? I'll give you a hint—it's not a standing ovation or society's stamp of approval.

True worth: that deep, unshakable kind, comes from within. It's not about how many people validate us and is more to do with how aligned we are with our own values. By that, I mean when we show up in the world as our most authentic selves and live in a way that reflects what truly matters to us. That's when we feel the fullness of our own worth.

Unfortunately, society has a million ways of measuring success and not one of them relates to what is in our hearts. If we keep chasing external markers such as more status, more approval, more *"doing it right,"* we'll end up feeling exhausted, frustrated, and disconnected from who we really are.

We have to turn our ears and eyes inward so that we can draw closer in faith and closer to ourselves. You see, in the spiritual world, hearing isn't just about listening with our ears. It involves inner, spiritual hearing that creates an air of faith. The Greek word **akouo** means to hear, but it also implies listening to God's voice, which has the power to nurture faith within us.

So, I would like to encourage you to engage in **akouo** as we move ahead.

> *Physical reality is only a mirror. And whatever you define it to be; whatever you believe is most true, is what you get. So it's very important to pay attention to those beliefs and those definitions, for it is those and only those that create your physical reality experience.*
>
> *~ Bashar*

Identifying Moments of Value

Every day, we face moments that chip away at our sense of worth—little jabs that make us question if we're enough. It happens in the subtlest ways: a dismissive glance, an unanswered message, a comparison we didn't mean to make but did anyway. And before we know it, we're spiraling, searching for validation in all the wrong places.

But our worth isn't something to be granted or revoked by outside forces. Rather, we cultivate it from within. That's why self-reflection is so important—it helps us tune in to the moments that make us feel truly valued. With that in mind, I want to challenge you to slow down and notice when you feel:

- **Appreciated:** When did you last feel seen and acknowledged?
- **Competent:** What moment made you feel capable and strong?
- **Fulfilled:** When did you feel deeply connected to what matters most?

Take a breath and really sit with these questions. What was happening in those moments? Who were you with? What were you doing? These aren't just passing feelings; they're breadcrumbs leading you back to your truest, most authentic self.

And these feelings can come in the moments we least expect. In *Man's Search for Meaning*, Viktor Frankl shows us something extraordinary: that even in the depths of suffering, our values don't disappear. They become sharper, more defined. The fact that he was able to find a deep sense of worth and purpose even in the horror of concentration camps by connecting his suffering to a larger narrative of love and responsibility is incredible. (Frankl, 2006)

Frankl's story reminds us that our worth isn't tied to circumstances; it shines brightest when tested. And while we can't always control what happens to us, we can control how we define it. No situation, by itself, dictates how we feel—our interpretation does. That might sound radical, but think about it: the same event can break one person and strengthen another. It's not the reality itself; it's the meaning we attach to it.

We only have to look at the remarkable life of Nelson Mandela to grasp how powerful this mindset is. Everyone knows about his terrible 27-year-long incarceration during the apartheid era in South Africa. Before being imprisoned, Mandela was already an influential man, but nothing could have prepared him for the hardships he was to face in Robben Island Prison. Hard labor, isolation from other prisoners, and restrictions on visitations must have taken their toll. But he continued in the struggle against oppression from within his cell walls, never allowing his circumstances to break his spirit. What I find most compelling about Mandela's story is his decision to forgive his oppressors.

I still recall to this day the momentous freedom walk on his release from the Victor Verster Prison in 1990. He himself stated, *"As I walked out the door toward my freedom, I knew that if I didn't leave my bitterness and hatred behind, I'd still be in prison."* Mandela never lost sight of what truly mattered and continued to strive for peace and reconciliation instead of revenge and hate, despite all of his suffering.

If your mind has the power to shape your experience in ways that diminish you, it also has the power to shape it in ways that uplift you. *Instead, start noticing those moments of recognition—the ones that remind you of who you are and what truly matters.*

Exercise 2: Identifying Moments of Recognition

Let's take a moment to reflect on and identify those significant instances when you truly felt recognized and valued. This exercise will help you understand what makes you feel worthy and how to create more of these amazing moments in your daily life.

Step 1: Reflect on Past Experiences

1.1. Recall Positive Moments

Take a moment to think back to times when you truly felt seen and valued. Not just when someone complimented you, but those deep, resonant moments when you knew you mattered. Maybe it was a time when your hard work was recognized, when a friend showed up for you, or when you made a real difference in someone's life.

<u>Example prompts:</u>

- When did someone acknowledge your hard work or achievements?

- Can you remember a time when a friend or family member expressed their appreciation for you?

- What moments in your life made you feel truly seen and heard?

1.2. Describe the Context

For each moment, describe the context in which it occurred. What were the circumstances? Who was involved? How did you feel at that moment? Be as detailed as possible to capture the essence of these experiences.

Example prompts:

- What was happening in your life during this time?

- Who played a significant role in making you feel valued?

- How did the recognition impact your self-esteem and overall mood?

Step 2: Analyze and Understand

2.1. Identify Common Themes

Look for common themes or patterns in the moments you described. Are there specific types of recognition that make you feel most valued? Is it praise from a superior, a heartfelt conversation with a friend, or achieving a personal goal?

Example prompts:

- What types of recognition resonate most with you?

- Are there certain people or environments where you feel more valued?

- How do these moments of recognition align with your values and strengths?

2.2. Recognize Your Contributions

Consider your contributions in each of these moments. What actions or qualities led to the recognition? Understanding your role can help you identify your strengths and areas where you naturally excel.

Example prompts:

- What did you do to earn the recognition?

- How did your actions reflect your core values and skills?

- What strengths did you display during these moments?

Step 3: Cultivate Future Recognition

3.1. Set Intentions

Based on your reflections, set intentions to create more moments of recognition in your life. Think about ways you can actively seek or cultivate these experiences. This could involve setting personal goals, communicating your needs to others, or simply being more mindful of your achievements.

Example prompts:

- What steps can you take to seek out recognition in your daily life?

- How can you communicate your need for appreciation to those around you?

- What personal goals can you set to create opportunities for recognition?

3.2. Practice Self-Recognition

While external recognition is valuable, self-recognition is a game-changer. Celebrate your wins, even the tiny ones and start making self-recognition a habit. The more you acknowledge your own efforts, the more you reinforce the truth: Your worth isn't up for debate. It's already there.

Example prompts:

- How can you build a habit of self-recognition?

- What daily practices can help you acknowledge your own worth?

- How can you celebrate your achievements, big or small?

When do you feel most seen for who you truly are? And when do you feel reduced to a label, an expectation, or someone else's version of you? These two questions can crack open a deeper understanding of your worth, if you're willing to sit with them.

The Challenge of External Judgments

Going back to Mandela, no doubt he would respond to these questions by saying his actions always reflected his values. It was never about personal glory for him, but about serving others. In the past, he was labeled as many things—a criminal, a terrorist, and even just a prison number. By his own admission, he was simply a man doing what he believed was right. Perhaps that's the greatest challenge we all struggle with: to remain true to ourselves.

External judgments are tricky. They sneak in through a colleague's off-hand remark, a family member's unsolicited advice, or the endless noise of societal expectations telling us who we *should* be. If we let them, these judgments can take up too much space in our minds, making us second-guess ourselves, shrink to fit someone else's comfort, or even disconnect from our own truth.

But here's the real question: *Where do these external judgments come from, and why do we give them so much power?*

Let's take a look.

Family and Friends	Workplace and Colleagues
The people closest to us can sometimes have the most significant impact on our self-worth. Their expectations, opinions, and comparisons can shape how we view ourselves. While their intentions may be good, these judgments can sometimes feel like pressure to conform to their ideals.	Professional environments are breeding grounds for external judgments. Performance reviews, peer evaluations, and even casual comments can make us question our abilities and worth. This can be particularly challenging when striving to meet job expectations or climbing the career ladder.
Cultural and Societal Norms	**Educational Institutions**
Societal standards and cultural norms play a big role in how we perceive ourselves. These unwritten rules about how we should look, behave, and succeed can create unrealistic benchmarks. Failing to meet these standards can lead to feelings of inadequacy and low self-worth.	Schools and universities often emphasize grades, test scores, and accolades, which can lead to a fixed mindset. The pressure to excel academically can overshadow personal growth and self-worth, making us feel valued only for our achievements.

What can we do about it?

One effective approach comes from Carol Dweck's research in *Mindset: The New Psychology of Success*. In her book, the renowned psychologist and Stanford University professor talks about the difference between a fixed mindset and a growth mindset. When we see ourselves as evolving and capable of growth, rather than being stuck with fixed traits, we almost instantly enhance our sense of intrinsic worth. This can override the noise of external judgments.

Shifting from a fixed mindset to a growth mindset involves changing the way we perceive our abilities and potential, and I'll explain just what I mean by that. Instead of believing that our talents and intelligence are static traits—or things that we cannot change—we start to see them

Seeing the Value Within

as qualities that can be developed through effort and persistence. For example, if you think you are inherently bad at drawing, adopting a growth mindset means understanding that with practice and the right techniques, you can improve. In this case, you would begin by engaging in activities you've never tried before, like taking a drawing class. As you start making progress and notice your skills improving, you'll reinforce the belief that you can learn and excel at new things.

Now, let's have a look at some of the other growth mindset ideals as compared to those of a fixed mindset.

Growth Mindset	Fixed Mindset
Belief in Development	Belief in Fixed Abilities
Embrace Challenges	Avoid Challenges
Persist Through Setbacks	Quit After Setbacks
Value Effort	Effort Dismissed
Feedback Welcomed	Feedback Resisted

Of course, part of having a growth mindset means that we have to believe in ourselves. The question isn't, *"Is it possible?"* We already know we can through the body of research and experience of having good things happen to ourselves and others. The question is, *"Is it probable?"* based on our current imaginings, thoughts, assumptions, and beliefs.

When you ask, *"Is it possible?"* you're looking for evidence in the world of dead thoughts and effects. Instead, ask, *"Who do you say I am?"* You have to strengthen that inner voice muscle and start being daringly confident in your ability to achieve. You can rise above anything that you feel is a blockage to your growth and worth if you just start seeing disadvantages as gifts.

This happens all the time in sport, where athletes consistently excel even after injuries or personal tragedies. A great example of this is when the University of Louisville Cardinals were playing an NCAA game against rival Duke University. Just as the then Sophomore player Kevin Ware was jumping up to block a shot, he landed very badly on his leg, breaking it in six places.

It was so painful and difficult to watch that even his teammates had to turn away and cover their eyes. They couldn't deal with the horrific sight before them. While Kevin was being carried off the court on the stretcher, he kept yelling over and over, *"Beat Duke! Win the game!"* An interviewer approached him on the sidelines and asked, *"Do you think you'll ever play basketball again?"* Kevin looked at her and replied, *"Oh, absolutely. Of course I'll play basketball again. This was just a minor setback for a major comeback."*

What I like about this story is it's a reminder that failure is never final and neither are setbacks when taken in a strategic comeback stride.

The Gift of Being Disadvantaged

See a disadvantage as a gift! I must be crazy, right? Hear me out for a minute. Society tries to remind us of our shortcomings. But reminding ourselves of our differences as inherent strengths allows us to see ourselves in a more whole and defined view.

When you see yourself, it allows you to authentically see and connect with others. It gives you the ability to treasure others.

Answer this: What if our greatest disadvantages are actually our most significant strengths? Consider attributes like sensitivity or introversion, which are often seen as drawbacks. These traits can be incredible assets that lead to deeper empathy, creativity, and thoughtful leadership.

Reevaluating these qualities can transform them from perceived weaknesses into sources of unique strength. This means that not only are we in a position to learn from those who have turned their struggles into triumphs, but we can also learn from ourselves. We can look as far back as our childhoods to draw the gems of knowledge from those experiences that we may have once suppressed or brushed aside.

For instance, someone who struggled with dyslexia as a child might develop exceptional problem-solving skills and creativity to navigate their reading and writing challenges. What was once a source of frustration and self-doubt can become an incredible foundation for innovation and resilience in adulthood. Richard Branson, founder of the Virgin Group, is a good case in point. Instead of allowing his dyslexia to hold him back, he taught himself to think outside the box and simplify complex problems. His story is a powerful reminder that perceived weaknesses can be transformed into unique advantages.

Similarly, a person who once felt isolated due to their introversion might discover that this very trait allows them to excel in solitary or more focused work environments where deep thinking and concentration are prized. That was certainly the case for J.K. Rowling, author of the *Harry Potter* series. She has described herself as a deeply introverted person, yet her introspective nature helped to create an imaginary world that would eventually bring her bestselling status.

Embracing our so-called disadvantages allows us to step into our authentic selves. When we accept and even celebrate these parts of us, we no longer see them as hindrances. Instead, they become a much-needed part of our unique contributions to the world. This shift in mindset can lead to greater self-acceptance and fulfillment because it allows us to align more closely with who we truly are and what we can offer.

Here's what I would like you to do. When you find yourself lamenting a perceived shortcoming, try to see it from a different angle. What strengths can you uncover within it? How can it contribute to your growth and success? By reevaluating your disadvantages, you will transform them into powerful tools for personal, professional, and even spiritual development. There's no two ways about it.

There is a reason why I would like you to focus on these 'disadvantages.' The reason is that you're already doing it anyway.

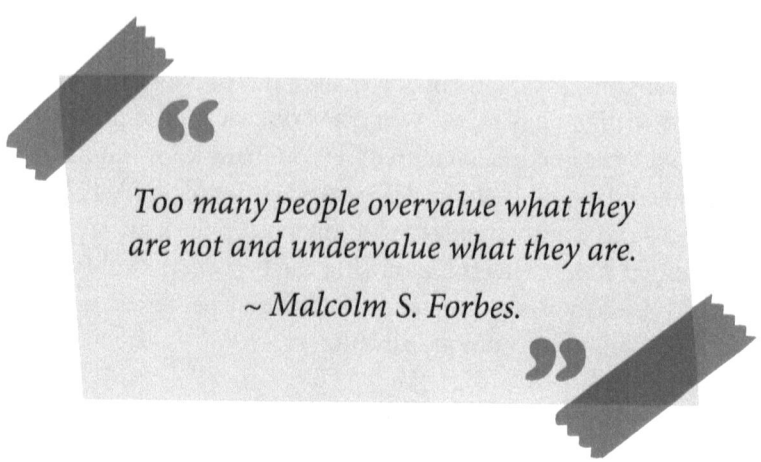

> *Too many people overvalue what they are not and undervalue what they are.*
> ~ Malcolm S. Forbes.

The human mind's tendency to focus on the negative, including our flaws and shortcomings, is actually part of a well-documented phenomenon known as the 'negativity bias.' (Vaish, 2008) This bias has deep evolutionary roots. Our ancestors needed to be highly attuned to potential threats in their environment to survive. If they failed to notice and respond to dangers like predators or hostile individuals, it could result in death. As a result, the brain developed mechanisms to prioritize negative information over positive information.

Neuroscientific studies have shown that the brain's amygdala, which processes emotions, is more sensitive to negative stimuli than to positive stimuli. This heightened sensitivity ensures that we quickly recognize and respond to those potential dangers I just mentioned. Negative events generally demand greater cognitive processing and engage broader neural networks than positive events. As a result, we spend extra time thinking about and analyzing negative experiences, which can reinforce the negativity bias.

To top it all off, our society and culture often emphasize caution and risk aversion. Negative news and information are more prominently featured in the media because they tend to be more effective at capturing our attention. Bad news is the best news, as they say in that line of business. But this constant exposure can further entrench our tendency to focus on the negative, which feeds into our negativity bias. Very soon, our minds are swamped with fear and negative memories that are then remembered more vividly and accurately than positive ones. And there's a reason for that too! The brain's hippocampus, which is involved in forming memories, works closely with the amygdala to consolidate emotional memories. (Yavas, 2019)

If your brain already has a proclivity toward the negative, you might as well give those disadvantages of yours the spotlight and reframe them in a way that works for you. When you embrace the side of yourself that you have cast aside for the longest time, you will see that you are worthy *with* your flaws. You might even begin to feel worthy *because* of your flaws.

Key takeaway:

It's our natural gifts and character combined that shape our success in life; how we use them can truly be make or break. As we learned in this chapter, having a growth mindset instead of a fixed one can help us reach long-term contentment.

Are you going to learn from your failures and come back even stronger or stay stuck in old patterns of thought, unable to move forward? I guess you already know which of the two options are more rewarding.

There will always be setbacks; times when you feel like the entire world is against you, or that you aren't good enough. It's in such moments that you can pool your inner strengths, backed by your core values. Failures then become lessons, and obstacles are there to jump over. Through introspection and deep thinking, you can grow as a person, all the while embracing your inherent gifts and strength of character. Think about it: your true worth doesn't lie somewhere out there. It's here, within you!

I know external judgments can be damaging, especially when everyone else seems to be doing great while we don't feel the same. These voices can overtake our sense of self, reducing us to dopamine-addicts, always seeking validation from the outside world. When this happens, we are disconnecting from our own truth and allowing others to define us.

So what if someone doesn't meet society's ideal of perfection? It didn't stop people like Richard Branson and look at his career trajectory to date. I think it's fair to say that many people thrive **because** of their difficulties and **not** despite them. Setbacks can make us adapt, become more resilient, and forge our own unique paths in life when we see each challenge as an opportunity for growth. Let's not forget that our flaws aren't our enemies—they can be our assets.

Think about the challenges you've faced to date and the natural strengths you possess. How has your mindset helped you to navigate deep waters, or prevented you from leaving port? Now is the time to take advantage of the rising winds to fill your sails and chart a new course. When you trust in yourself, you can set sail toward the horizon of your making with renewed confidence and purpose.

CHAPTER 3

THE DESIRES THAT DRIVE US

"You are more powerful than you know; you are beautiful just as you are."
— Melissa Etheridge

We all have needs that must be met. Some of them are unique to each individual's journey, while others are universal. Recognizing our worth and understanding how this fits in with our personal desires is one of them. At the same time, we all seek love, security, respect, purpose, being heard, and mattering, whether aware of that or not. More importantly, how we go about fulfilling these needs in the grand scheme of our stories is the key to contentment.

Take love, for example. Some find it in romantic partnerships, others in deep friendships, and some in the passion for their work or creative expressions. On the other hand, security might come from having a stable job, a strong social network, or a deep spiritual conviction. We all want to feel respected, find a purpose, be heard, and know that we count. How we fulfill these needs influences the path we take, and it's this path that influences who we become.

With that in mind, it's important to explore the commonalities or benchmarks that make us truly human, beginning with our values.

Values and Their Origins

Our values are rooted in our deepest desires and the gaps we've experienced in our lives. Think about it: the thing that you value most often fills a void you've felt at some point. If, for example, you've ever experienced the feeling of being neglected by caregivers or a significant other, you might value attention highly. If you've experienced chaos, then you might value stability. These past voids, along with the virtues you hold dear today, create the foundation of your personal values, but it's not enough simply to acknowledge them. You need to build a vision that aligns with them, one that will guide your choices and actions. Being in tune with your values is what gives your life a sense of purpose and direction.

I'll give you Muhammed Ali as a prime example.

If you weren't already aware of it, the world-renowned boxer was originally born as Cassius Clay in 1942, later changing his name to Muhammad Ali after his conversion to Islam. But it wasn't merely a change of name: it was an all-encompassing transformation of the self. This new identity was anchored in his values of confidence, determination, and excellence, which he embraced wholeheartedly, allowing them to shape his thoughts, actions, and beliefs.

One of the most significant cultural figures and sportsmen of all time, Ali is well known for saying, *"I am the greatest."* He allowed all assumptions and beliefs to form around this new identity. In fact, he later reflected on this statement, saying: *"I said I was the greatest before I knew I was."* This belief in himself was so great that he spoke success into existence. In the process, he detached from the old reality and rose in consciousness to his new identity.

You might be wondering why I mention excellence, since I have done nothing but go against the grain of perfectionism from the outset. Well, there is a major difference between excellence and perfectionism. Perfectionism wants you to be better than everyone else. Excellence wants you to be better than you were yesterday. So, Ali's belief in himself wasn't unfounded bravado or bragging, It was rooted in that pursuit of excellence, in years of hard work, training, and a deep understanding of his craft. Ali recognized that to achieve greatness, he had to see himself as great first. This gave him the power to rise above the challenges he faced and prove that he really was *'the greatest'* in the ring.

To understand the impact of our gifts, we need to develop self-awareness. Everyone has certain inclinations and talents. Yes, they are not inherent, meaning we're not born with them as I mentioned a moment ago. However, these gifts can really propel us forward in life and career when they're honed correctly. They make the hard stuff seem easy and the impossible suddenly seem achievable. But gifts alone aren't enough for lasting success. They can open the first door, but it's character that opens the rest – and keeps them open.

Building on this, creating a clear vision based on your values requires deep honesty, which might initially feel uncomfortable. Depending on how deeply ingrained your negativity is, it can take weeks or even months to begin thinking differently and aligning with your true values. This process demands consistent practice and conscious effort, which is why it's crucial to explore not only what you value but why you value it. Once you understand that, the next step is integrating those values into your everyday life. When you can answer that, the work will feel incredibly worthwhile.

Dr. Caroline Leaf, a renowned neuroscientist, has researched lasting mental change and the formation of new habits. She emphasizes that building enduring change in thinking takes approximately sixty-three days, a process she calls the *Neurocycle*. This method involves consistently practicing new habits and thought patterns, helping to reprogram our brains and make these changes permanent.

According to Dr. Leaf, in the Neurocycle, we should practice our new habit at least seven times per day to embed it in our unconscious minds, making it automatic.

By day twenty-one of the cycle, we will have established a new long-term memory for the behavior or event. With regular practice, these changes will become more ingrained. This is a powerful tool for creating new habits that reflect our values, especially during personal growth.

Leaf's research on neuroplasticity shows that this process not only helps form new habits but can also identify the root causes of issues like burnout, anxiety, and trauma. By tracing these signals back to the underlying thoughts and mindsets, we can disrupt the neural networks that trigger unhealthy responses. This allows us to deconstruct old patterns and reconstruct them into healthier ways of functioning—all within 63-day cycles.

Through this process, we can reframe our thinking, build new habits, and align our behaviors with our values in a lasting and meaningful way.

For example, if you struggle with guilt about self-care, begin by identifying the underlying belief that it's selfish. Challenge that belief by affirming that self-care is essential for your well-being and helps you support others. Over 63 days, practice this new mindset at least seven times a day. By day 21, you'll create new long-term memories, and by the end of the cycle, self-care will become a natural, guilt-free habit aligned with your values.

Let's take a look at how you can begin to define your values.

Exercise 3: Defining Your Values

Figuring out your core values is a crucial step in embracing who you are. When you are aware of them, it's much easier to align your actions with them. This exercise will help you pinpoint what truly matters to you and how to live in accordance with those values.

Step 1: Reflect on Your Core Beliefs

Take a moment to reflect on what you believe in deeply. Think about the principles and standards that guide your decisions and behavior. Write down at least five core beliefs that you hold.

Step 2: Identify Your Values

Once you have defined your core beliefs, try to identify the values that emerge. By values, I mean the qualities and standards that you strive to embody in your daily life.

Here are some examples to get you started:

- Integrity
- Compassion
- Excellence
- Honesty
- Creativity

- Loyalty

- Respect

- Courage

Step 3: Prioritize Your Values

Once you have identified your values, it's helpful to prioritize them. Which ones are most important to you and why? Rank them in order of significance, starting with the one that is most important to you.

Step 4: Reflect on How You Live These Values

Now, consider how you currently live out these values in your everyday life. Are there any areas where you could improve? And what about any values that you have neglected? Take the time to write a brief reflection on how each value manifests in your life, and where you would like to make changes.

Step 5: Set Intentions

Based on your reflections, setting clear intentions for how you will live according to your values can be a game-changer. Make sure that these intentions are specific and actionable. For example, if one of your values is compassion, you might set an intention to volunteer at a local shelter once a month or to practice active listening in your daily interactions.

Step 6: Create a Values Statement

You can summarize your values and intentions in a values statement. This should sum up who you are and what you stand for. stand for. It serves as a kind of personal manifesto that you can refer back to whenever you need to remind yourself of your core principles.

Here's an Example of a Values Statement:

"I am committed to living a life of integrity, compassion, and excellence. I will approach every situation with honesty and creativity, striving to be loyal and respectful to those around me. I will face challenges with courage and maintain a positive attitude, knowing that my values guide my actions and decisions."

When you define your values and align yourself with them, you will find that you are able to fulfill those necessary human desires without being misled by them. Your values will serve as a beacon that guides you through every aspect of your life. You can find love, without allowing toxic relationships to lead you away from your morals, faith, or sense of self. You can pursue success without sacrificing your integrity, and build deep friendships based on trust and respect. Your values stand as a reminder of your self-worth and can guide your decision-making, whether that's in your relationships, your career, or your own personal growth. In short, they help you to stay true to your authentic self.

Influence of Resources

The pursuit of happiness can often keep us trapped in misery. It's ironic, really, that chasing after something so joyous can often bring us a lot of pain. The real problem here lies in our expectation of happiness. The Dalai Lama teaches us that happiness isn't something we just find ready-made. Rather, it comes from our own actions, which need to be in line with our inner values. This perspective is a clear reminder that real happiness is something we create from the inside out through the choices we make and the way we live our lives. (Lama, 2009)

He also discusses the importance of developing a sense of compassion and mindfulness. You may wonder what these two traits have to do with our own happiness. Compassion means genuinely caring about the well-being of others and wanting to help them when they're struggling, as well as sharing in their joy. When we practice compassion, we build positive connections with the people around us, which in turn makes us feel happier and more fulfilled. Mindfulness, on the other hand, is about staying present and fully experiencing each moment. It helps us stay grounded and focused, which reduces stress and makes us feel more at peace. Instead of worrying about tomorrow, we can cultivate an appreciation for being in the present moment and experience a sense of contentment.

In a nutshell, the Dalai Lama suggests that true happiness comes from having deep connections with others and a sense of inner peace. When we form meaningful relationships and treat others with kindness and understanding, we enrich our lives with love and support. This gives us a sense of belonging and security, which are essential for our emotional well-being.

We humans are hardwired for companionship and being part of a tribe, which goes back to our early days as hunter-gatherers. Back then, being part of a group wasn't just a nice-to-have for our ancestors: it was a matter of survival. Living in tribes protected them from predators and hostile groups, as well as making hunting and gathering food more efficient. Beyond that, it ensured there were enough hands to raise children and support the elderly. For that reason, people who were good at forming bonds and cooperating with others had a better chance of surviving and passing on their genes.

You could say that, in essence, our brains are wired for this social life. We know that when we interact with others, our brains release chemicals like oxytocin and dopamine, which make us feel happy and connected.

Ever wondered why hanging out with friends or loved ones can be so rewarding? Now, you know the answer to that. It's like our brains are giving us a gold star for being social and shows that belonging to a group is a must for our psychological health. We are social creatures, and it's a well-known fact that isolation can lead to feelings of loneliness and depression (Cacioppo & Patrick, 2008). Our need for social interaction is so strong that prolonged social isolation can make the brain perceive it as physical pain (Eisenberger, Lieberman, & Williams, 2003). This just goes to show how important it is for our mental well-being to have companions and a sense of community.

Finally, having a tribe gives us a sense of identity and belonging. It helps us understand who we are and where we fit in the world, which boosts our self-esteem and overall psychological health (Jetten, J., Haslam, C., & Haslam, S. A., 2012). Belonging provides a support network during tough times and a group to celebrate with during the good times. Surprisingly enough, all of this gives us a great foundation to live and think independently because when we have strong roots (support systems), we are less fearful of spreading our wings.

Having a strong sense of self means we won't be so tempted to focus solely on the material world and our base desires as a source of worth. This is what gives us the staying power we need to live a fulfilling and rewarding life.

It all boils down to these intrinsic motivators and how they play a role in our important human needs as opposed to the common ones. Daniel Pink's *Drive* highlights this perfectly in the context of career because it shows us that what motivates us is often an intrinsic drive that transcends monetary rewards or external recognition. (Pink, 2011) Pink explores the concepts of autonomy, mastery, and purpose as the key drivers of motivation. He argues that when we find work that aligns with our values and which gives us a sense of purpose, we are more likely to be engaged and satisfied. It's an important insight when considering how our values influence our actions and overall satisfaction in life.

Seeking out activities and goals that resonate with our deeper sense of purpose rather than just chasing resources or material gain are much more beneficial to our overall sense of worth and happiness. This approach helps build a belief system and worldview that brings us closer to recognizing our inherent worth.

Belief Systems and Worldviews

Belief systems and worldviews are like the glasses we wear, shaping our view of the world and influencing our understanding of worth. Such systems include religious beliefs, cultural norms, and personal philosophies – all of which affect how we see ourselves and others. When we talk about worth, it's important to recognize how these belief systems impact our sense of value and our common human desires. So, let's get back to that, as we only touched on it earlier in the chapter. We all have fundamental desires such as love, security, respect, purpose, being heard, and feeling like we matter. These desires are universal and cut across cultures and belief systems. But the way we go about fulfilling these needs can vary a lot depending on our belief systems and world views.

Love is a good example. In many cultures and religions, love is seen as a fundamental virtue. Christianity emphasizes agape, or unconditional love, which fits in with our deep desire for meaningful connections. Meanwhile, some Eastern philosophies focus on universal love and compassion for all beings. Despite these differences, the basic human need for love and connection is the same.

When it comes to security, different belief systems offer various ways to feel safe. Many religions promise spiritual security and protection, which can bring comfort and peace of mind. On a more secular level, cultural norms and societal structures provide security through laws, social systems, and community support. This sense of security is vital for our well-being.

Then we have respect, which is another universal desire that shows up differently depending on one's world view. In some cultures, respect is closely tied to family and social hierarchies, while in others, it's earned through personal integrity. Regardless of the cultural context, we all want to feel respected and valued. However, rather than believing we desire to feel respected and valued by others, what we really want is to feel those things toward ourselves.

In the end, belief systems often give us a sense of purpose by offering narratives and goals that align with our values. Many religious doctrines outline paths to fulfillment through service, devotion, or enlightenment. Similarly, secular philosophies and spiritual paths might emphasize personal growth, contributing to society, or pursuing knowledge as ways to find purpose. No matter how we find our sense of purpose, it offers us enough faith to rest along the way—to not be weary in waiting, as we'll discuss later—and to find meaning in our lives without having to be constantly productive or busy.

This is all rooted in our desire to be heard and to matter. However, before we seek recognition from others, we must first learn to hear and value ourselves. Life isn't about external validation or end goals. As the old adage goes, the pursuit of the Holy Grail is far more important than the grail itself. It's the journey that shapes us—the beliefs, perspectives, and experiences along the way—that count.

By recalibrating these initial steps, we can reconnect to our true character and, therefore, our true worth.

Key takeaway:

Living a fulfilling life starts with aligning our actions with our core values. It's all about being self-aware and practicing mindfulness and compassion to stay grounded and connected to our true selves. Instead of aiming for perfection, we focus on striving to be better than we were yesterday. It takes time to build new habits and challenge negative beliefs, but it is possible with consistent practice to grow into the best versions of ourselves.

While things like love, security, respect, and purpose are universal needs, the way we go after them is often based on the beliefs we hold and the society we live in. The key takeaway here is that true happiness doesn't come from external validation but from within.

When we connect with our core values and let them drive us, rather than focusing solely on the end goal, our sense of self-worth aligns beautifully with our authentic selves.

CHAPTER 4

CHARACTER AND GIFTS

"You are what you do, not what you say you'll do."
— *Carl Jung*

Imagine this: you've got an amazing gift for something you're naturally good at. It could be painting, coding, writing, or public speaking. This gift opens doors, creates opportunities, and even brings you into the spotlight. That's fantastic, right? I would like to think so, but here's the problem: if your character doesn't match up with your talents, things can start to unravel pretty quickly. Your gifts can shoot you into the stratosphere, but it's your character that keeps you there (or not).

So, what exactly is character?

Think of character as the foundation of a house and your gifts as the structure. Without a solid foundation, no matter how beautiful the house, it's vulnerable to collapse under pressure. Your character is the energy that remains when you leave a room. It's the set of mental and moral qualities that define who you are, even when no one else is watching. It's the guiding force behind your actions and decisions, shaping how you respond to different situations in life.

More than that, your character hinges on integrity, honesty, courage, and the commitment to do what is right, even when it's difficult. The beautiful thing about character is that, like talent, it's not something you are born with, but it develops over time. Every choice you make, every action you take, the way you treat others, and how you show up in the world, forms character. If you consistently choose to be honest (even when it's inconvenient), you will build a reputation for trustworthiness. When you act with kindness and empathy, you will develop a compassionate character.

In that sense, character really is like a muscle. The more you exercise it by making good choices, the stronger it becomes. But how does this tie in with natural gifts?

Natural Gifts and Their Impact

To understand the impact of our gifts, we need to develop self-awareness. Everyone has certain inclinations and talents. Yes, they are not inherent – meaning we're not born with them, as I mentioned a moment ago. However, these gifts can really propel us forward in life and career when they're honed correctly. They make the hard stuff seem easy and the impossible suddenly appear achievable. But gifts alone aren't enough for lasting success. They can take us up to the first level, but it's character that elevates us even higher and keeps us there.

Take Michael Jordan, for instance, often regarded as one of the greatest basketball players of all time. Jordan was undoubtedly gifted with

Character and Gifts

incredible athleticism and natural talent. However, it wasn't just this raw talent that made him stand out—it was his relentless work ethic and determination to improve. Jordan famously didn't initially make his high school varsity basketball team but, instead of giving up, he used that setback as fuel to work even harder. He practiced relentlessly, always pushing himself to improve his skills, both on and off the court.

Michael Jordan's success wasn't just due to his natural gifts, but the result of his mindset and commitment to continuous growth. He recognized that talent alone wouldn't get him to the top; it took discipline, resilience, and the willingness to put in the work, even when it seemed like the odds were stacked against him.

This mindset—one that embraces effort, growth, and perseverance—is what allows people to rise above challenges. Whether facing personal setbacks, professional roadblocks, or criticism, it's our character that will carry us through. It's how we respond to adversity and how committed we are to our long-term goals that will define our success.

As much as achieving success is important, maintaining it is where discipline and consistency matter. Michael Jordan once said, *"I've failed over and over and over again in my life, and that is why I succeed."* Talent may open the first door, but it's our character, shaped by hard work and a growth-oriented mindset, that ensures we keep walking through it.

While Jordan's story shows how resilience and work ethic can elevate natural gifts into lasting success, the golfer Tiger Woods journey offers a cautionary tale of what can happen when character doesn't align with talent.

Tiger Woods is a gifted golfer who became a world champion at the age of 21. This victory marked the beginning of his dominance in the sport, winning a total of 15 major championships and achieving a record 683 weeks as the World No. 1 ranked golfer during his career. When his personal life began to unravel due to struggles in his marriage, his golfing career took a nosedive. Despite breaking barriers in the traditionally white sport of golf, Woods involvement in a public scandal in 2009—including a car crash and the revelation of multiple affairs—shattered his image.

His admission of infidelity and subsequent fall from grace marked a sharp contrast to his once-perfect public persona.

The loss of endorsements, a costly divorce, and a series of injuries seemed to signal the end of his career. But in 2019, Woods made a remarkable comeback, winning The Masters and regaining the support of many fans who admired his determination to move on from his past mistakes. His redemption story reinforces the lesson that talent alone can only take us so far—it's character that sustains us through challenges and allows us to grow from our failures.

Success and Setbacks Based on Character

How do you know if you're relying too much on your natural talents, or if you're truly cultivating growth through consistent effort while staying aligned with your values? This is where self-awareness comes into play. It's about honestly assessing whether your reliance on talent has led you to overlook the importance of character and hard work, or if you are actively developing both aspects of yourself.

Self-awareness means being in tune with yourself and really understanding the reasons why you think, feel, and behave as you do. It takes bravery to have an honest look at who you are, what drives you, and how your actions reflect your true values. But self-awareness is also the key to seeing yourself clearly, so you can make choices that are aligned with how you want to show up in the world.

Are you using your natural abilities as an excuse to coast? Or are you actively working on developing your character and mindset, even when it feels uncomfortable? These are good questions that require honest reflection, feedback from those you trust, self-assessment, and setting intentional goals.

Let's break that down with some prompts you can reflect on:

Character and Gifts

1. **Honest Reaction**

    When you stop and look at your thoughts, feelings, and reactions, you will develop more clarity. Ask yourself:

    ◊ Do I rely too much on my natural talents when things get tough?

    ◊ Do I avoid hard work because I know I can get by on my abilities?

    ◊ Why do I react badly when I fall short?

You might feel a little bit uncomfortable with these questions but as psychologist Tasha Eurich (2018) points out, only about 10-15% of people are truly self-aware. It's only by digging deeper into your motivations and actions that you can grow and learn.

2. **Feedback from Others**

    We all need feedback from others to help us become more self aware. Think of it as a gift, even if it sometimes feels painful. Ask your friends, colleagues, or mentors:

    ◊ Do you think I play it safe or rely on my strengths too much?

    ◊ How do you think I could improve?

    ◊ Do I show up in difficult situations?

Real feedback might be bruising but it will help you to build greater self-awareness. And when you learn, you grow.

3. **Journaling and Self-Assessment**

    Journaling is a great way to build self-awareness as it allows you to express clearly your experiences, thoughts, and feelings. Writing can even help you make sense of everything, reduce stress, and simply make you feel better.

- ◊ Some journaling prompts to use are:
- ◊ What did I accomplish today and how much of my character or talent played a role in that?
- ◊ What challenges did I face today that forced me to look at my responses more carefully?
- ◊ What did I do today that reflected my values?

Journaling is a kind of inner dialogue with yourself that gives you a chance to spot the good and bad patterns in your behavior. It's then a lot easier to see where you need to improve.

4. **Setting Intentional Growth Goals**

   Growth doesn't come along by accident and you need to put goals in place if you want to achieve anything. They should be actionable and specific, not pie-in-the-sky dreams that are unlikely to materialize.

   For Example:

   - ◊ Set a goal to meet up with friends or family at least once a week, even when you think you don't have time.
   - ◊ The next time you have a conversation, try to listen more intently to the other person and resist the urge to react. Just listen!
   - ◊ Set a goal that aligns with your core values, even if it might be inconvenient or unpopular.

The more we practice this kind of self-awareness, the more we build a life that reflects who we truly want to be. It isn't just about recognizing our strengths; it's also about understanding the deeper qualities that shape how we live and interact with the world around us.

Character and Gifts

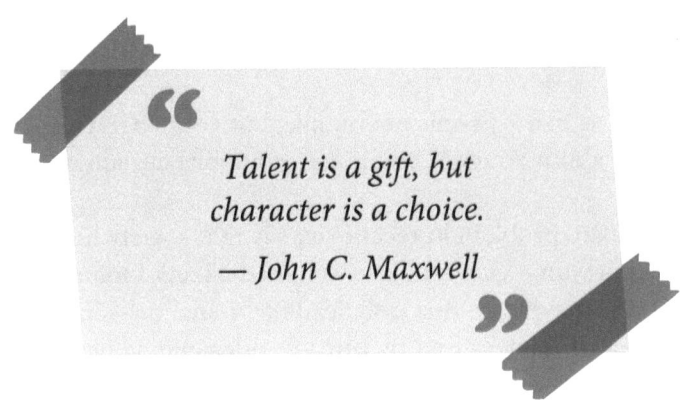

> Talent is a gift, but character is a choice.
> — John C. Maxwell

This brings us to an important distinction that helps us navigate growth: character. In essence, character is made up of developed virtues. In *The Road to Character*, New York Times columnist and author, David Brooks, talks about two types of virtues.

First, there are 'resume virtues.' These are the skills and achievements we showcase to the world; the things that get us jobs and promotions. Think about qualities like ambition, productivity, and professional success: all important qualities that help us advance in our careers. But, Brooks says, they don't truly define the richness of a person's life. (Brooks, 2016)

Then there are 'eulogy virtues.' These are the qualities people remember and talk about at our funerals. They include kindness, bravery, honesty, and loyalty. These virtues reflect our inner character and how we treat others. Brooks believes that these are what truly define who we are and the legacy we leave behind.

Someone known for their kindness might have built meaningful relationships and created such a positive environment that their kindness is remembered long after any professional achievements are forgotten. Bravery is a quality that lets people stand up for what is right. Honesty builds trust and respect in all relationships. I could go on, but the point is that character—those virtues that we've developed over the years—are what will add to our sense of self-worth.

The Role of Introversion in Character Building

You can fool as many people as you like, but your character will shape how you feel about yourself when the proverbial curtain closes.

The unfortunate problem in recent years is that society has us focused too much on resume virtues; that instrumentalizing I mentioned in the Introduction. Inevitably, this only leads to a shallow sense of worth, where our value is measured by our job titles and achievements. But true fulfillment comes from developing eulogy virtues—the qualities that make our lives richer and more meaningful.

This isn't a new dilemma. Philosophers have been discussing the nature of character, virtues, and morality since ancient times. Most great thinkers of the past stressed the importance of inner virtue and a life built on integrity rather than accomplishments. From Aristotle to Confucius and Jesus Christ to Buddha, the pursuit of moral and intellectual virtue has always been seen as the key to one's happiness.

Traces of this ancient wisdom can still be found today high on the sunny slopes of Mount Parnassus in central Greece. On the walls of the Temple of Apollo at Delphi—the navel of the world—is the inscription, 'Know thyself.' Socrates referred to this idea in Plato's *Apology*, stating that it's the only way for us to live a life of fulfillment. The notion of self-awareness involves focusing on our inner growth instead of external achievement and it's a trend we still find today in the realm of self-development.

In fact, most of the New Age philosophies and self-help schools are based on these ancient ideas. Concepts like emotional intelligence, mindfulness, and 'discovering your true self' have their roots in classic principles, reminding us that true success isn't only about *what* we do. It's also about who we *become*.

How can you develop these virtues? You can begin by looking inward and reflecting on your values and actions. Start by asking yourself a couple of questions:

Character and Gifts

1. When have I felt most proud of myself, and what values were reflected in those moments?

2. How do I treat others when no one is watching, and what does that say about my character?

3. What difficult decisions have I made that required me to act against my own immediate interests for the sake of a greater good?

When you have the answers, they'll point you in the right direction of your virtues, which are similar in nature to your values. From there, you can align them with your gifts. But first, it's important to establish what those gifts are.

Exercise 4: Exploring Your Natural Gifts

Objective: The aim here is to identify and understand your natural gifts so you can leverage them more in your personal and professional life.

Step-by-Step Guide:

1. Reflect on Your Childhood Interests

- Spend a few minutes thinking back to your childhood. What activities did you naturally gravitate toward? Write down any memories of what you loved to do and what you were passionate about as a child.

2. Identify Activities That Make You Lose Track of Time

- Think about the present. What activities do you find yourself so absorbed in that you lose track of time? List these activities and consider why they engage you so deeply.

3. Seek Feedback from Others

- Ask three people who know you well—friends, family, or colleagues—to share what they think your strengths and natural gifts are. Write down their responses and look for common themes.

4. Notice What Comes Easily to You

- Reflect on tasks or activities that come easily to you but might be challenging for others. List these tasks and think about what skills or talents are involved.

5. Explore Your Passions and Hobbies

- Consider your current passions and hobbies. What do you love to do in your free time? Write down these activities and note any skills or talents they require.

6. Take a Skills and Strengths Assessment

- Consider taking a formal assessment to identify your skills and strengths. Tools like the CliftonStrengths or VIA Character Strengths Survey can provide valuable insights into your natural gifts. Summarize the results and reflect on how they align with what you've discovered in the previous steps.

Character and Gifts

In the long run, your gifts will only keep serving you if you cultivate a strong character. Your talents are the tools you use, but character is the toolbox where they're kept. So, how can you nurture your character?

First, let's talk about emotional intelligence (EQ). You've probably heard of IQ, which measures how smart you are, but EQ is equally important. It's about understanding and managing your own emotions, as well as being able to read and respond to others' emotions. Imagine coming home after a stressful day and your partner starts unloading about their own troubles. Without emotional intelligence, you might snap or retreat into frustration. But if you're emotionally intelligent, you'll pause, listen, and offer empathy. By being emotionally aware, you can handle tough situations without letting them escalate.

Another way to nurture your character is through resilience. Life is full of ups and downs, and things won't always go the way you expect. Challenges, disappointments, and failures are part of the human experience. But resilience isn't just about *"bouncing back"* in the traditional sense; it's about adapting, learning, and growing from the experience. When something goes wrong, resilient individuals don't let it define them. Instead, they see obstacles as opportunities for personal growth.

For example, think of a time when you faced a significant challenge—maybe a project didn't go as planned, or a personal setback put you on the back foot. How did you handle it? Did you shut down and let it defeat you, or did you find ways to learn from it and keep moving forward? Resilience is often about maintaining a positive mindset even when circumstances are tough. It's knowing that while you might not be able to control every outcome, you have control over how you respond. And every time you rise after a fall, you build your resilience muscle, making you stronger and more capable of handling whatever life throws your way.

It's also essential to seek feedback, even though it can be uncomfortable. Sometimes, we don't realize how our actions affect those around us until someone points it out. I had a recent experience like this with a friend. I'd been so wrapped up in work that I didn't notice I was dominating our conversations, leaving little room for him to share what was going on in his life. When he told me how that made him feel, it was eye-opening. The feedback wasn't easy to hear, but it helped me grow. When we invite others to share their perspective, it can make us more aware of how we show up for them and help us to adjust when we're falling short.

Doing the right thing, even when no one is watching, is a core part of building strong character. Integrity is about making choices that align with our values, regardless of the outcome or recognition. Take Keanu Reeves, for instance. He's known for his humility, and he demonstrated it in a big way during *The Matrix* trilogy. After the success of the film, he took a significant pay cut to ensure the crew was better compensated. This wasn't about publicity; it was about doing what he felt was right. Integrity might not always get you the spotlight, but it builds a reputation that lasts.

Finally, helping others is one of the most powerful ways to nurture character. It doesn't have to be grand gestures; even small acts of kindness can make a huge impact. When we give to others, whether through our time, knowledge, or just our presence, we are strengthening not just our own character, but also that of the community around us.

Developing greater emotional intelligence, resilience, integrity, and kindness are character-building qualities that will support you through the ups and downs of life. And as you grow in these areas, your talents will shine even brighter, and the foundation beneath them will be solid.

Key takeaway:

When you fully understand your natural gifts, you can begin connecting the dots. Do you think that your success or setbacks could be linked to how you use your gifts? Do you believe you could have achieved more based on your talents? If you do, it might be a character-related issue that is holding you back from reaching your full potential. This could also be diminishing your sense of self-worth

By combining your natural gifts with strong character, you can create something truly valuable. Much like a master craftsman

who also takes care to maintain and sharpen their tools, nurturing both your gifts and character is key to building a fulfilling and impactful life.

CHAPTER 5

DITCH THE FEAR

"There is no illusion greater than fear."
— Lao Tzu

It's 3 a.m. and your mind is racing. Sleep is an escape artist, leaving you wide-eyed, staring into the darkness as worry steps in. Damn it! You said something inappropriate today; you forgot to send that important email; you don't know if you can cover your expenses this month. As night turns into dawn, you toss and turn, knowing exhaustion awaits you tomorrow. The more you fret, the less you sleep, then anxiety decides to drop in before you're even out of bed. It barges through the door and starts rearranging the furniture before making itself at home on your sofa.

I don't know about you, but when anxiety and worry show up, they completely take over my brain, body, and mood.

As for addiction, that's often our go-to place when we want to silence the internal noise and dumb down our thoughts and feelings. Whether it's scrolling, shopping, eating, drinking, gambling, or sex, there are plenty of ways for us to avoid discomfort.

You may put anxiety, worry, and addiction down to your personality type, or chalk them up as inconvenient habits, but I assure you there is much more going on below the surface.

Anxiety, worry, and addiction all relate to how worthy we believe ourselves to be–how much we value our self-worth. You see, when we don't believe we are good enough, these behaviors move in, becoming unwelcome house guests we just can't get rid of. But what if we could break free of this cycle? What if we exposed anxiety and addiction for the imposters they really are: not uncontrollable forces but responses to pain we can change?

Let's rewrite the narrative and learn how to evict these destructive roommates from our lives.

Understanding the Roots of Anxiety

Why is it that when life throws us a curveball, we don't just stress out, but we also begin the self-blame game? *Did I bring it on myself? Am I at fault? Did I mess up?* These thoughts don't just pop into our minds; we welcome them with open arms and pass them a microphone.

In reality, anxiety isn't only about stressful situations, although they can be the triggers. More often than not, it's long-held beliefs we have about ourselves that are the underlying cause: *I'm not good enough. I'm the problem.* As soon as things start to go wrong, we allow anxiety to take over, turning stress into a vicious cycle of rumination, self-blame, and emotional burnout.

But there's more. Low self-worth is also connected to chronic anxiety. When we don't feel we are 'enough', we live in a constant state of hypervigilance, which plays out in our minds. It's as if we are just waiting for the moment we will say the wrong thing, let someone down, or fail to achieve a goal. How many times have you asked yourself: *Did I say something stupid? Have I upset someone? Did I make the wrong move?*

I'm sure you know how exhausting it can be if you can relate to this kind of anxious over-analysis. It's also a hard habit to break when you have been in this mode for a long time. It tells you your worth is conditional, based on how well you perform, how much you please others, or how few mistakes you make. In short, you've set the conditional bar too high, making it impossible to clear. Worst-case scenario? You fail, which is a terrifying thought, since that will confirm what you secretly believe about yourself in the first place: *You aren't capable. What a disappointment!*

Anxiety affects people in all walks of life, from those at the top to everyday folk. When a public figure confesses to suffering from anxiety, it highlights the problem even more, proving that it's a very human response. There are plenty of examples in the sporting world of athletes struggling with anxiety and Naomi Osaka is one of them.

A four-time Grand Slam tennis champion, Osaka has talked openly about feeling overwhelmed by the intense pressure of the game and being in the public spotlight. This led her to eventually withdrawing from the French Open in 2021 for mental health reasons. Osaka's decision to put her well-being first sparked a global conversation about the whole mental health issue in sports, especially for Black athletes.

The research backs up the fact that low self-worth and anxiety go hand in hand. One significant study showed that low self-esteem doesn't just *accompany* anxiety—it causes it. (Sowislo and Orth 2013) Think of low self-esteem as a vulnerability factor: when you see yourself as unworthy, you're more likely to view life through a negative lens. When curveballs come along, as they undoubtedly will, it's likely that you will interpret them as confirmation of your worst fears. A relationship issue, a career setback, or a financial struggle, all lead to one conclusion: you are not enough, you are unworthy. It's no wonder that this negative mindset makes you feel anxious and if it increases, can lead to further anxiety and other mental health issues. It's a slow burn when you set off on this path, as persistent feelings of low self-worth affect your whole take on life.

How do we tend to manage these feelings of anxiety? By overthinking every move, micromanaging our actions, and trying to dodge rejection, shame, or disapproval. It's a constant drain, leaving us exhausted before we even begin. I'm sure you don't want to live like that., which is why it's time to address these issues.

Let's get something straight: there's no need to prove your worth to anyone. It's in your hands to reframe your negative thought patterns and banish anxiety from your life once and for all. You don't have to earn your value, you already possess it!

Exercise 5: Who are you?

Take a moment to reflect on these questions, which will change how you view yourself:

1. **Measuring Self-Worth**

   How do you measure your worth? Is it based on what people say about you or how you think they see you?

2. **The "Should" Trap**

   Do you often find yourself saying that you *should* be better at something or *should* act differently?

3. **Challenging the Inner Critic**

   Write down some of the things your inner critic tells you. Would you say those things to a friend?

4. **Reframing Mistakes**

   When was the last time you feared failure? How could you reframe that experience as an opportunity for personal growth?

5. **Self-Compassion**

    How often do you practice self-compassion? Try writing a comforting note to yourself, free of self-judgment and criticism.

We usually feel like anxiety is uncontrollable when we experience it. After all, it seems to show up out of the blue, even when we think we are calm and composed. That's because anxiety is a sophisticated response our brains have developed over thousands of years to keep us safe. It's the fear of the saber-toothed tiger, even though they no longer exist. But it's not so easy to override such a primal survival instinct. The brain's safety system can go into overdrive, putting us on high alert all the time, even when there's no real or present danger around.

Why does this happen? Think of a highly trained first response team, with the amygdala in the driver's seat. This part of the brain processes emotions, triggering the alarm whenever it senses danger–a bit like a smoke detector. Now, our amygdala has undergone millennia of evolutionary training and is specialized in spotting perceived threats. Once it does, it signals to the HPA axis (that's the hypothalamic-pituitary-adrenal axis), which releases stress hormones like cortisol and adrenaline. (Ressler & Mayberg, 2018) We are now in a fight or flight state, ready to respond by fighting or fleeing the perceived danger.

The trouble is this reaction is often unnecessary (no saber-toothed tigers spotted today), so you end up reacting to things that aren't life-threatening at all. For example, having to speak in public or take an important exam aren't dangerous but they can still get your heart racing and cause dizziness. Anxiety feels automatic and uncontrollable.

Fortunately, despite all of the brain's hard-wiring, you can control how it reacts. Practices like mindfulness, self-awareness, and therapy, can train your brain to respond differently. It's about fine-tuning those automatic reactions so that they activate only when necessary. Not an easy process, I admit, but one that is absolutely doable.

Exercise 6: Managing Anxiety

1. **Recognize the Trigger:** Acknowledge the anxiety right away and say to yourself: *"Okay, I'm feeling anxious because my brain is perceiving this conversation as a threat. We're just having a disagreement, and I'm not in danger."*

2. **Stop to Breathe:** Before you respond, take a few deep breaths. Breathe in deeply, hold it for four counts, then exhale for four. This is a simple action to help calm the body, shifting from fight-or-flight mode to a more calm state.

3. **Reframe the Situation:** Rather than seeing the argument as a sign the relationship is collapsing, reframe it by saying to yourself: *"This is just a disagreement, and I can work through it. It's normal for disagreements to arise from time to time and it's not a threat to the relationship."*

4. **Communicate Mindfully:** Once your body and mind are calm, you can approach the conversation with a clear, open mind. Instead of anxiety steering your reactions, you can express your thoughts honestly and say something like: *"I'm feeling a bit overwhelmed right now. Let's take a short break and come back to this when we're both calm."*

5. **Practice Self-Compassion:** Hey! Feeling anxious during an emotional conversation is completely human

> so don't beat yourself up over it. Show yourself some self-compassion instead by saying: *"It's natural that I feel anxious now but I'll get through this."*

Imagine you have a disagreement with a close friend or partner, and it begins to escalate out of control. Notice that your heart races, your throat tightens, and your mind fills with anxious thoughts. This is the amygdala on high alert, reacting just as it would if you were facing real danger.

When you reduce intense emotional reactions and allow space for a more calm and constructive conversation, you can beat anxiety. Practice this strategy long enough and you will become a master at navigating difficult emotional situations without letting the first responder take over.

There is a connection between how we cope with anxiety and fear as adults and our early childhood experiences. As babies, we rely on our primary caregivers to survive, and it's this dependency on others that forms our attachment styles. To illustrate this point, let's look at two examples:

First, take a child who grows up surrounded by warmth, attention, and reassurance. The parent or caregiver is there to soothe them whenever they feel distress, fear, or discomfort. This teaches the infant that comfort is available, stress and fear are temporary, and that they can rely on others to support them. Once the child reaches adulthood, they are more capable of dealing with anxiety without losing balance, knowing that challenges can be managed with the help of others.

On the other hand, imagine a child growing up in an unpredictable environment, where the primary caregivers are not always affectionate, and might be dismissive or even absent. A child that is met with indifference when they need comforting will learn that their emotional needs aren't always met. This can lead to feelings of insecurity, which also manifests as anxiety and fear of rejection. By the time they reach adulthood, they may feel they have to prove themselves to be loved.

Such early childhood experiences shape our attachment styles, which ultimately affect how we cope with stress, especially in relationships. Attachment theory was first formulated by British psychologist John Bowlby in 1982, who noted that when children experience secure attachments, they are more likely to develop a sense of trust and emotional regulation. But when those early attachments are inconsistent, it can lead to anxiety, fear of rejection, and an overwhelming sense of never being good enough. (Bowlby, 1982) In our first example, you could say that the child develops a secure attachment style. The child in our second example could develop what's known as an anxious attachment style.

Early conditioning can teach us that love and approval are conditional. Perhaps you only received praise growing up when you performed well at school or achieved something. That could have led you to believe that you are only worthy when you are successful or meet other people's expectations. And now, you have made the equation in your head that self-worth=validation. You might find yourself constantly striving for perfection, fearing failure, or feeling anxious about disappointing others.

This overlaps with perfectionism—the belief that only when you are perfect will you be worthy of love, acceptance, and even respect. That's a crazy thought, considering that perfection is almost impossible for anyone to achieve. Nevertheless, many of us have been brought up to think that perfection earns love and this idea invades the way we live as adults. It manifests itself through our inner critic—the voice in our head that loves to constantly remind us of how we are not good enough—probably never will be. Trying to meet impossible standards is certainly one way of being in a constant state of anxiety, don't you think?

But believe me, your worth isn't something you have to earn. It's not tied to achievements, accolades, or approval of others. You are inherently valuable, just as you are.

I recall visiting an old friend of mine who had a successful law firm. His office was covered from wall to wall with awards, diplomas, and framed recognitions—a visible testament to his hard work and accomplishments. Yet, as we sat down to talk, and I congratulated him on his success, he sighed before confessing something unexpected: *"No matter how much I achieve, or how many big cases I win, I never feel like I'm enough."*

His words struck me deeply. Despite the external validation reflected in his numerous achievements, he still felt a void inside—a sense of never measuring up. This, I realized, was the painful truth: his constant search for external approval was fueling an internal anxiety that no amount of recognition could satisfy. In his case, the more he sought validation from others, the deeper the emptiness became.

I believe this internal void can only be filled when he begins to build his own self-worth, independent of others' perceptions. Only when he learns to acknowledge his intrinsic value, without needing to prove himself through accomplishments or recognition, will he be able to truly say, *"I am enough."* Until then, it's very likely that he will remain trapped in a cycle of external validation and self-doubt.

So, how can we deal with anxiety? Once we understand its root causes, we can take the first steps toward healing. This allows us to change the narrative of our inner critic. We have to understand that our childhood conditioning is not connected to our adult reality, and release the pressure to be perfect. Instead, we can find value in simply being human. Self-acceptance is a gradual transformation that requires patience, self-compassion, and some soul searching, but it is achievable.

Here's a guide to help you on your way:

1. Identify Your Core Beliefs About Yourself

Your unconscious beliefs about yourself are based on your early experiences, and these continue to influence how you deal with stress and anxiety. Feelings of inadequacy or fear of rejection may well come from those early years, burying themselves deep within your psyche.

You can get a clearer idea of where these beliefs come from by asking yourself the following questions:

- What kind of things did you hear often as a child? Did you only receive praise when you performed well at school? Or were you praised for trying hard, regardless of the result?

- What thoughts rush through your mind whenever anxiety overcomes you? Do you tell yourself, *"I'm not good enough. I need to do better to be loved"*?

- Do you equate worth with achievement or success?

2. Reflect on Your Early Caregiving Experiences

Try to think back to your younger days and recall how your caregivers responded to your needs. Being surrounded by secure, consistent love fosters confidence, while being raised in unpredictable circumstances can lead to anxiety and self-doubt.

- Were you comforted when you were upset, and made to feel loved and supported?

- Did you receive consistent support from your caregivers or were they often unavailable emotionally, withdrawing their love or approval?

- Did it feel safe to express your emotions or were you taught to keep them in?

3. Recognize How You Respond to Stress and Rejection

The way we were raised has a significant impact on how we cope with stress, criticism, and rejection in adulthood. When caregivers are critical or distant, that can create self-doubt as we grow. We might feel the need to people-please or be perfect in order to earn approval.

- Do you tend to judge yourself harshly when you make a mistake?

- Do you often find yourself over-apologizing or feel responsible for the way others feel?

- Do you see asking for help as a weakness?

4. Notice Patterns in Your Relationships

Once we have developed a certain kind of attachment style, that can influence how we relate to others. Unstable early experiences, for example, might mean that we struggle with insecurity in our relationships.

Some of the signs to watch out for are:

- Seeking constant reassurance from others and fearing they might leave or stop loving you.

- Struggling to set boundaries and worrying that by saying *"no,"* others might reject you.

- Pushing people away when they get too close, afraid of being vulnerable or losing your independence.

When we understand these patterns, it becomes a lot easier to separate our conditioned responses from our present reality and help us to build relationships based on trust instead of fear.

5. Shift the Narrative of Your Inner Critic

The inner critic is often the voice of our childhood fears and doubts. Think of the times you were scolded, criticized, disapproved of, or simply ignored. If you can challenge these thoughts, you can gradually erase anxiety and self-judgment.

- Ask yourself, *"Would I speak to a friend this way?"*

- Instead of saying *"I must be perfect to be loved,"* try *"I am worthy as I am."*

- When you feel anxiety arising, remind yourself, *"This is an old pattern, but I am safe now."*

6. Practice Self-Awareness and Healing Strategies

It may be relatively easy to pinpoint the conditioning we have experienced. It's quite another thing to create a new way of thinking. Some of the daily practices that can be useful to help achieve this are:

- **Journaling:** Writing about your childhood experiences can help you to unlock what shaped your fears and beliefs. Explore what messages you received from your caregivers about self-worth or how they responded to your emotional needs. You may be surprised at how much insight you can gain into the way you are now.

- **Mindfulness:** Since anxiety is often anchored in past fears or future worries, mindfulness helps because it invites you to focus on the present. This can be a great way to switch off from intrusive thoughts that have a negative effect on your sense of worth.

You can't heal from childhood conditioning overnight but you can start to break the cycle. Begin by noticing the patterns you've carried with you from the past and start challenging them. Eventually, you can change the soundtrack you have been playing over and over in your mind about how unworthy you are.

Every time you catch yourself slipping back into self-doubt or a desire to be perfect, you will find it easier to press the pause button. In time, you will realize the only truth that counts: you are already enough, just as you are. This takes off the pressure to be perfect and reduces that relentless feeling of anxiety that keeps you up at night.

Breaking the Cycle of Worry

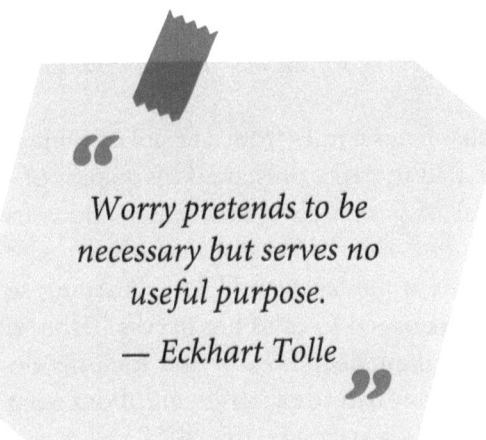

> *Worry pretends to be necessary but serves no useful purpose.*
>
> — Eckhart Tolle

You know that worrying about something doesn't bring any solutions, right? Worry isn't a problem-solving exercise. It's more likely a trap that gets us stuck in an exhausting anxiety loop. So, why do we do this to ourselves, and how can we get out of it?

When tossing and turning at night, fretting about a problem or replaying a conversation, it's easy to get stuck in *repeat* mode. Going over the details a zillion times solves nothing. Although worrying might create the illusion that we are in control–that we can fix a problem–it doesn't actually work. It's like waiting for a train when we are already running late—no matter how hard we stare down the platform, it's not going to arrive any faster.

Psychologists like Borkovec (1998) explain this through the *avoidance theory of worry*. Thinking long enough about a problem won't prevent bad outcomes. All that occurs is overthinking leads to paralysis, waiting for the worst-case scenario to happen.

What's the alternative? How about *productive thinking?* Unlike worry, productive thinking makes us focus on *actionable steps*—what we can do to solve a problem. Instead of having a mental breakdown about what might go wrong, we shift our attention to what we can do about it.

If you're worried about getting to work late, worry probably sounds like: *"I'm going to be fired. My colleagues will think the worst of me."* On the other side of the coin, productive thinking sounds like: *"I'll make up for the lost time, and remind myself my boss and colleagues value me."*

A great example of this comes from a friend of mine who used to freeze every time she had to make presentations as part of her job. Standing up in a room full of people always made her a nervous wreck. Her head was full of thoughts like: *"What if I make a mistake? What if I sound like I don't know what I'm talking about?"* After learning some mindfulness techniques, she managed to calm her nerves before each presentation. It was as easy as taking deep breaths and focusing on the sensation of her feet on the floor. Instead of obsessing about what could go wrong, she changed her inner narrative to: *"All I have to do is talk about a topic I'm familiar with. That's it."*

Even well-known artists can experience the same turmoil before performing. Adele, one of the most successful female artists of our time, has talked a lot about the anxiety she faces before going on stage. According to the singer, this anxiety comes from her fear of being *"found out"* as not being good enough. Such an extreme reaction may include experiencing panic attacks and sensations of nausea. Worry, even for celebrities and successful artists, can be debilitating.

The good news is that there are ways to deal with these responses. Mindfulness, which I mentioned above, is one of them. It's a very simple way to bring us to the *present moment*. Rather than focusing on the what-ifs in the future, it grounds us in *what* is happening right now

Research shows that mindfulness disrupts rumination–that constant chewing over things in our minds–and we can practice it anywhere. (Hoge et al. 2013) Instead of getting caught up in a state of worry, we can guide our thoughts toward something more useful. Here's a simple 3-step mindfulness exercise to try:

1. Take a slow, deep breath.

2. Notice how your body feels—your feet on the ground, the air on your skin.

3. Gently bring your attention back to the present whenever your mind wanders.

It sounds almost *too* simple to be true, but just try it. Over time, you can train your brain to let go of anxious thoughts and replace them with a calm mind.

If you really want to rid yourself of worry, there's nothing like some good old-fashioned self-compassion. Kristen Neff, who I mentioned in a previous chapter, is a leading researcher on this topic and has extensively explored its impact on well-being, claiming that when we treat ourselves compassionately, we reduce our levels of anxiety.

You might be asking, how can being kind to myself stop me from worrying? What's the connection? Well, apart from feeling better at that moment, you will be able to confront the problem with a clearer mind. To understand this more, we can break down self-compassion into three key elements that help to reduce anxiety:

1. Self-Kindness vs. Self-Criticism

2. Common Humanity vs. Isolation

3. Mindfulness vs. Over-Identification

Let's look at the first one, **Self-Kindness vs. Self-Criticism**. How we talk to ourselves matters. When was the last time you scolded yourself for making a mistake? You probably thought, *"Why did I do that? I'm an idiot!"* But there is a better way to respond, one that is much more beneficial. Instead, you could say to yourself, *"That was a mistake, but I'll learn from it."*

Despite thinking that self-criticism will make you do better next time, it can make you feel worse. Apart from creating even greater anxiety, it's a real blow to your motivation, getting you caught up in a vicious cycle of worry. (Gilbert, 2009)

Interestingly, when you treat yourself with kindness, this soothes the nervous system and the body's stress response. Oxytocin–the hormone responsible for making you feel safe and supported–is released, and this biochemical shift has long-term benefits. Over time, it strengthens your resilience, helping you to bounce back from setbacks and failures. (Neff & Germer, 2013)

In terms of **Common Humanity vs. Isolation,** it's easy to think we are totally alone in our struggles when we are going through a hard time. We convince ourselves that everyone else is doing okay while our own life is falling apart. A bit of self-compassion here can remind us that struggle is *part of being human.* And while we all make mistakes, what's more important is how we respond to them. That's another reason why connection is so crucial, especially in this day and age, where everyone seems to be in their own virtual world. When we connect, we see that everyone experiences setbacks, and become more open to seeking support. Not only that: we can extend our kindness to others and ease our own burdens. A problem shared is a problem halved, right?

When we recognize our common humanity, personal failures become shared experiences, and it's comforting to know we aren't alone. Such a simple shift in the way we think can take the pressure off and prevent us from worrying so much.

Finally, let's talk about **Mindfulness vs. Over-Identification.** It's so easy to get lost in worry that we don't see the big picture. If you think you are going to fail your driving test, there's a strong possibility you will, since you believe it without question. Instead, how about taking a step back and recognizing your anxiety are simply thoughts (and not truths) that you don't need to identify with? It's all about gaining perspective.

Practicing mindfulness helps to create space between yourself and your thoughts, allowing you to respond with clarity rather than react out of fear. Instead of being consumed by worst-case scenarios, you can acknowledge your worries without letting them define you. Think of small fluffy clouds floating by you high in the sky. Each one is a thought–simply let it pass. Over time, this shift will help you approach challenges with a calmer, more balanced mindset—one that empowers rather than overwhelms.

Overcoming Addictive Behaviors and Finding Peace

It isn't possible to go into every aspect of addiction in this book. However, understanding that addiction is a coping mechanism can help foster a mindset of greater self-worth.

As Gabor Maté, an expert on child development and addiction, mentions in his book; In the Realm of Hungry Ghosts: Close Encounters with Addiction (2008), *"Addiction is not a choice that anybody makes; it's not a moral failure. What it actually is: it's a response to human suffering."*

You may not have connected the dots about your addictive behavior and past experiences, but Maté suggests that it's the impact of trauma and stress that have a significant effect on our mental and physical health. Whether we drink too much, gamble, spend too much time on our phones, or do drugs, these addictive behaviors are ways of coping with unresolved emotional pain. (Maté 2008)

You are probably familiar with the actor Robert Downey Jr., who has struggled with addiction in his life. Being a celebrity meant he made the front pages every time he was arrested, and he was in and out of rehab throughout the 1990s and early 2000s. Downey has spoken candidly about his addiction, revealing how he was exposed and introduced to drugs from a very early age by his father. It became clear to him that his own drug use was a way of coping with unresolved emotional pain and personal struggles. Through rehabilitation, mindfulness practices, and strong personal support, the actor eventually managed to turn his life around. Downey is a great example of how addiction is often linked to deeper emotional wounds. He also shows us that, with the right mindset and support system, we can overcome.

How can you break free from addictive behavior? The first step is to become self-aware and pay attention to your patterns. What things do you do without thinking—things that have become habits? Once you pinpoint them, you will see that they aren't serving you anymore.

Let's take online shopping, for example—a common, and seemingly harmless, habit these days. I know many people who spend hours browsing online stores when they feel stressed. It's an easy habit to adopt. If you've had a bad day at work, fallen out with a friend, or just feel down, scrolling through your phone and adding items to the basket can make you feel better in that moment. By being more mindful of what you are doing, how much time (and money) you are spending, you will discover that your emotional energy is being funneled into unhelpful behavior. It's this kind of self-awareness that can help you to break the cycle and find healthier coping strategies for your stress. A walk in the park, a bike ride, reading a book, or going for a swim are all better ways to deal with overwhelm after a hard day.

Don't get me wrong: this type of emotional regulation isn't about swallowing your feelings or ignoring them. It's more about learning how to process your emotions in a healthier way and consciously deal with them. If you can achieve this, it will become a lot easier not to give in to harmful urges and impulses.

You may have fallen victim to addiction because you don't believe you deserve any better. If you have an 'unworthy' mindset, or think you don't deserve to be happy, it can be difficult to break free from harmful behavior. The truth is that having a greater sense of self-worth can aid recovery. Instead of buying into the idea that you 'need' to do something, you can start to see it as a choice—you can choose to continue on that destructive path or choose to have a healthier life. When you believe in your own value and worth, you will be less tempted to throw that away for a quick fix.

Here are three key steps to building a worthiness mindset:

- **Practice self-compassion:** I've already talked about self-compassion and being kind to yourself when you slip up. The less you self-criticize, the less likely you are to fall into negative patterns of behavior linked to addiction.

- **Surround yourself with positive influences:** On those days when you feel low and struggle to see your self-worth, surround yourself with people who can support you. Even if you are hard on yourself, friends and family can rally around to bolster your self-esteem. Seek them out whenever you need to.

- **Set small, achievable goals:** Take each day as it comes and avoid setting yourself impossible goals or expectations. Celebrate each success, no matter how small, as you reinforce your sense of worthiness.

One of the most effective ways to overcome destructive behavior patterns is by replacing them with healthier alternatives. Physical activity, meditation, and journaling can all be incredibly therapeutic. The next time you feel anxious or stressed, instead of reaching for the bottle, pick up a book, do some gardening, play with your cat—whatever it takes to break the cycle. I can guarantee you that the more you do this, the more in control you will feel of your reactions.

Key takeaway:

Anxiety and worry are outdated survival mechanisms: meant to protect us but often redundant in modern life. Studies show that most of what we worry about never happens: 91% in fact. (Leahy, 2005) Despite that, our brains remain wired to potential threats, getting us caught up in the overthinking loop.

But if you struggle with low self-worth, worry is also a sign of your internal fears. Your brain will work overtime to find reasons why you might fail, be rejected, or fall short. Add anxiety and self-doubt to the mix, and you end up believing you are incapable of handling life's challenges.

Here's the thing: Worry is a tool, not a truth. Since most of your fears never materialize, perhaps most negative beliefs about yourself are also illusions. Challenge your fears, doubts, and self-perception to shift the narrative in your mind. You are already worthy, trust me!

CHAPTER 6

CHANGE IS POWER

The only constant in life is change."
— Heraclitus

Change can be traumatic, life-changing (for better or worse), and very scary. What will happen if our familiar lives suddenly go haywire! How will we cope, and what will our future hold?

No one likes to go through change. We all prefer to sit in our lane and avoid having to deal with events that force us to step outside of our comfort zone. Even if we are certain that change is for the best, we are resistant. Why? Because we are creatures of habit. We love routines, familiarity, and predictability. When our life goes as we expect it to, we feel safe, secure, certain. As soon as things begin to unravel, well, panic sets in as we feel like the rug is being pulled from under our feet.

Our natural inclination is to resist change. Letting go of the familiar and stepping out into the great unknown feels risky, dangerous, and often terrifying. There is something unnerving about it that triggers our deeply-rooted survival instincts. Our desire for the familiar makes sense in evolutionary terms, since it keeps us safe. Wandering off the beaten path to uncharted territory has always had its risks. Who knows what dangers may lie ahead–we may get lost or even be devoured by a wolf!

You might be stuck in an unhappy marriage but choose to stick it out because the alternative doesn't bear thinking about. Perhaps you hate your present job but 'better the devil you know…,' right? Very often, though, change is thrust upon us: a sudden illness or injury, a serious accident, a financial loss, or the death of someone dear. We can't always control our circumstances–changes are going to happen whether we like it or not. The fallout can be equally devastating if we are unsure how to handle it: loss of confidence, loneliness, not to mention physical and mental health issues.

How can we see change for what it is–inevitable–and learn to grow from it instead of going under? What mindset can we adopt to adopt change and allow ourselves permission to be a little messy in the process?

Navigating Life's Transitions

In his book *Transitions: Making Sense of Life's Changes (2004)*, William Bridges explains that real change happens inside us when we are faced with shifting sands. He talks about the three psychological stages we go through: the ending (where we let go of the old), the neutral zone (the messy middle space where we feel lost), and the new beginning (where we start to move forward). Once we understand these three stages, we can be a little kinder to ourselves when it all seems like one big mess.

That's exactly what the author Bruce Feiler talks about in his book *Life Is in the Transitions: Mastering Change at Any Age.* (2020). Feiler's main take on the subject is that life doesn't follow a linear path. Instead, we all experience what he calls *"lifequakes"*—big, often unexpected changes that shake us up. His research gives us insights into how we can respond to these quakes and learn to thrive through them.

First, we have to accept that life quakes are inevitable: we will experience three to five of them during the course of our lives. That could be in the form of divorce, illness, or other personal challenge. It could also be a collective event, such as the COVID-19 pandemic or an economic slump. Every lifequake involves a transitional period, which Feiler describes as *"the long goodbye, the messy middle, and the new beginning."*

What came out of Feiler's research is that people who actively reshape their personal narratives are more resilient. The stories we tell ourselves can help us to rewrite our identities, moving from being a passive victim to someone who can control their life. It's the small steps we take that help us to adapt, rather than making dramatic changes. The smaller the steps, the more control we can have of the outcome.

Here's an example of what happened to a friend of mine that highlights this approach:

Rachel hated her job as an accountant but was too afraid to make that move into the unknown. You could say this was the ending stage; letting go of the familiar. Thinking about all of the things she would miss—her colleagues, the predictable routine, the clients—filled her with uncertainty about the future. Even though she desperately wanted to branch out on her own, she was afraid. What if she failed? What if she regretted leaving a stable income behind?

At first, Rachel had no clear plan, only that she had to make a change. She second-guessed herself constantly, wondering if she had made a terrible mistake. Friends and family didn't help much either; their well-meaning questions only made her doubt herself more. *What are you going to do now? Is this really the right time to start over?* She felt lost, adrift in an identity crisis she hadn't anticipated.

But instead of letting regrets and insecurities prevent her from moving forward, Rachel embraced the unknown. She had always had a passion for cooking and had dreamed of running her own baking workshops.

This was her new beginning phase, where she started organizing herself with a different career in mind. She took online courses, connected with people who had started their own businesses, and began hosting trial workshops from home.

After a slow start and a few sleepless nights filled with self-doubt, Rachel was determined to push through. As her courses gained more participants, she began to feel more confident of her abilities. Her actions were driving her success; she never had a perfect plan. It was her willingness to persist through the messy middle and meet uncertainty with adaptability, grit, and resilience that brought her the rewards she desired. Rachel got why she needed to go through these changes, and that made it easier.

Whatever happens, change helps us to grow as a person. Once we see that, the resistance subsides.

Having a growth mindset, which I talked about in Chapter 2, is imperative if we want to handle change successfully. It stems from the idea that, rather than being a catastrophe, change can be a learning experience if we choose to see it that way. While Rachel found the idea of walking away from her full-time job daunting, she came out of it with a renewed sense of purpose and fulfillment. It's never an easy path, but there are definitely gains to be made when we go for it.

Of course, not all change is welcome or expected. While some transitions, like Rachel's, involve a leap of faith, others—such as the loss of a loved one—shake us to our core. I know this pain firsthand, having lost my brother. Nothing could have prepared me for the grief I experienced, coupled with feelings of anger. Bereavement is a terribly dark place to abide; an abyss that isn't easy to climb out of.

We owe it to ourselves to mourn fully but, in time, we also deserve to find a way forward, each in our own way. It takes courage to accept and move on, with the healing process unfolding differently for each individual. I don't have a magic trick up my sleeve to help anyone who is grieving for someone they lost, but I can say that death is part of life. It's a seismic change, for sure, and the aftershocks can be felt for a long time to come. It's one of life's most difficult transitions and we can decide how to carry it with us as we move forward.

Change occurs whether we like it or not, and always has done. There is no such thing as an uninterrupted lifespan, and, to be frank, that would be quite boring. We are always in a process of transition, from growing up to leading grown-up lives. Events happen, whether personally or collectively: the world changes, people change, our environment changes, seasons change, dreams change. On a personal level, we shift gears, move in different directions, sometimes change speed, and set our sights on new destinations. Collectively, we adapt, adjust, and accept new paradigms. Life doesn't exist without change so the more open we are to it, the better. When we navigate change with curiosity, courage, and self-compassion, we can explore new ways of being without getting lost along the way.

Buddhism teaches that impermanence (*anicca*) is one of the fundamental truths of existence. According to these teachings, suffering comes when we try to resist the inevitable: clinging on to a branch as the river's current pulls us downstream. This doesn't mean we must always surrender to the current without question. Rather, it's about recognizing when we're resisting out of fear versus when we're making an intentional choice to steer our course. It's more about understanding the difference between holding on out of fear and making a conscious choice to adapt.

Think of all the changes you have experienced in your life—some of them will have brought you discomfort because you preferred stability. Maybe you had to relinquish an old identity, a past relationship, a career, a certain lifestyle: hanging on to them out of fear would have only made it harder for you to move on.

What if I told you that change isn't just inevitable, but it's also essential?

Just like the transformation of a chrysalis into a beautiful butterfly, the shift can be liberating. We will go through many transitions in life and find ourselves in this chrysalis stage—that messy middle, where everything feels confusing and messed up. Yet, it's through this metamorphosis that we grow our wings, letting go of what was to experience what can be.

Sure, there will be fallout on the way—a loss of something we thought was permanent— and that's disorienting, but necessary. Transformation takes time and effort; we have to work through the hard parts and trust the process, coming out at the other end feeling lighter, freer, and ready to spread our wings.

Let's say, for example, you have to move to a new house. You are so used to calling the old one home that the thought of leaving is truly upsetting. It has been your sanctuary, haven, and place of security for so long that you are filled with angst and trepidation about the move. The idea of living in a new neighborhood is scary, too. You won't know anyone. You'll have to take a different commute to work. You aren't familiar with the area. All of these fears are resistance to change. And the more you resist, the more miserable you will become. If you can go with the flow, you will find the move less painful. Even though everything is uncertain, something new is on the horizon and when you embrace that, change becomes a welcome phase in your life.

In 1969, Swiss-American psychiatrist Dr. Elisabeth Kübler-Ross, published her groundbreaking book, *On Death and Dying*. She outlined the five stages of grief (denial, anger, bargaining, depression, and acceptance), widely known as the Kübler-Ross Model. Although it was initially developed to explain how we cope with loss and terminal illness, the model applies to all kinds of major life transitions. These include personal growth, career shifts, relationship break-ups, and even social changes. Whenever we face one of these events, we go through a kind of grieving for something we have lost, just in the same way we might grieve when we lose a loved one. There's a feeling of loss for the familiar, control, and even a loss of identity–who are we without our job, spouse, partner, home, or good health?

If we can understand this *Change Curve*, we can navigate transitions with greater self-compassion. I want you to take a look at the five stages more closely. Have you recently experienced any of these feelings after something changed in your life?

Change is Power

1. Denial: "This isn't happening."

Our first reaction is to resist reality, or try to convince ourselves that it's only temporary. If you've ever lost your job, you might talk yourself into believing it can't be possible–they must have made a mistake. There's a good reason why our brain behaves in this way: it's protecting us from the intense emotional impact that change can bring.

2. Anger: "Why is this happening to me?"

Once the dust settles and reality sets in, it's natural to feel frustrated. This might be expressed outwardly as anger, or inwardly as self blame. Shouting at your boss might seem completely justified at the time: they are responsible for your misery, after all. If you blame yourself instead, ruminating over perceived failings, this may also seem logical. The funny thing is, this response actually means you are grappling with the change, trying to make sense of it.

3. Bargaining: "Maybe if I just..."

We then move to the bargaining phase, where we try to negotiate our way back to the past. The *"what if"* and *"if only"* scenarios play out in our minds as we attempt to undo the damage. You may take the next job that pops up, even for a lower salary or position, as you try to get some stability back into your life. This is a natural attempt to regain control when things seem like they are out of our hands.

4. Depression: "I can't handle this."

Often, the bargaining phase doesn't work, and we are left to face the full reality of our situation. You might experience feelings of self-doubt, sadness, and loss. During this messy middle period, life can be one big question mark as we struggle with apprehensions at what comes next. And, guess what? This is when we begin the transformation as our discomfort forces us to let go and move forward.

5. Acceptance: "This is my reality, and I can move forward."

We don't have to love the change and it can still hurt, but at least, by this stage, we are not resisting it anymore. After thinking, *"Why did this happen to me?"* you come to a place of, *"What can I learn from this?"* It's here that you discover new ways of being, new possibilities, and, eventually, a new normal.

Acceptance doesn't happen overnight—it's a slow process that is different for each person. You may feel optimistic one day and then slip back into sadness or anger the next. As long as you get why this is happening and understand it's a necessary part of the process, you will be able to come out of it, wings intact!

The Power of Flexibility and Adaptability

Change forces us to master flexibility and adaptability. To successfully navigate the ups and downs of life, we need to be able to adjust our sails and harness the momentum. If we can manage this, we can ride any storm that comes our way.

I'd like you to think about a palm tree, which doesn't snap when it encounters a storm. It sways with the wind in an elegant dance, sometimes even touching the ground, only to rise again when the storm is over. It's resilient–able to endure extreme conditions without breaking. Watch any footage showing major storms making landfall and you will notice that everything in the storm's path is destroyed, apart from these amazing palms. How is this possible?

Palm trees are designed by nature to bear the brunt of hurricanes. With a fibrous, spongy trunk, they can bend without snapping. Their shallow but wide root system anchors them securely to the ground as the wind rages. Their long, narrow, and aerodynamic leaves bend to let the wind pass through rather than acting as barriers and palms grow from a single apical meristem (or crownshaft) protected deep within the trunk, helping them to regenerate easily. If palm trees can survive hurricanes by moving with the wind instead of trying to *resist* it, I think we can learn a lot about how to deal with change.

While the palm teaches us resilience, the apple tree offers another lesson: adaptability. You wouldn't say that an apple tree simply braces itself for the change in seasons—it adapts to them. Spring is the time for it to bloom, while summer helps to yield its fruit. Autumn ushers in the period of letting go as its leaves fall to the ground, with winter being a period of rest. The apple tree doesn't resist the changing seasons. It adjusts to the cycle of growth and rest, able to evolve in tune with the environment.

If we can be open to change in the same way, we make space for personal growth. In short, letting go of the past helps us to create a new tomorrow without fear of the unknown.

We need to be as flexible as a palm and as adaptable as an apple tree to successfully navigate change. So the next time you find yourself resisting, ask yourself: Where do I need to stand strong and where do I need to adapt?

I can think of many instances in my life where I've needed to stand my ground, despite the storm, to achieve my long-term goals. I'm not the same now as I was five, ten, or twenty years ago and the path hasn't always been easy. I've had to adapt through uncertain times to get where I am today. I often take inspiration from other people who have managed to weather the storm without losing sight of who they are and what they want. One such figure is the legendary Roberta Flack, who passed away in 2025 at the age of 88.

Despite being a household name, few people truly know the depth of Roberta Flack's journey. Even fewer are aware that she began her music career in classical music, and that she was considered to be a child prodigy. After earning a scholarship to study piano at Howard University when only 15, Roberta dreamt of becoming a concert pianist. But her early struggles with race and gender discrimination meant she had to rethink her musical aspirations. The limitations forced her to adapt, which she did beautifully, using her classical training in mainstream music of the day such as jazz, soul, and R&B. It's this exceptional ability to re-invent herself that made Roberta Flack such an enduring artist over the years.

From virtuoso to opera singer turned music educator, and a nightclub performer, Roberta eventually signed up with Atlantic Records in 1969. She went on to achieve 18 Billboard-charting songs and won 4 Grammy awards. Her versatility and innovative style allowed her to blend classical elements with folk, jazz, Latin, and Motown music, creating a unique repertoire that appealed to a wide audience. What set her apart from other artists was her amazing ability to bring great emotional depth to her music. She was also a strong supporter of collaboration, working with a large number of musicians and producers. Not only was she brave enough to try out different genres, but her collaborations with others helped her to remain relevant in the changing music industry. Despite the systemic racism and sexism she encountered, Roberta refused to be held back. She took control of her recording sessions, producing her own album—a bold move that showcased her determination and inner strength.

Roberta's story exemplifies what psychologist Angela Duckworth explores in *Grit: The Power of Passion and Perseverance* (2016). Duckworth argues that sustained effort and adaptability matter more to long-term success than raw talent or intelligence. In short, people who face obstacles head on and are willing to adapt are the ones who ultimately achieve success.

Roberta Flack's career is a great example of this. Recognizing the limitations black women faced in classical music, she adapted, and continued to re-invent herself without compromising her musical integrity. The artist showed great resilience when she experienced the loss of her friend and collaborator, Donny Hathaway. Devastated by the loss, she continued in her creative pursuits, honoring his legacy in her work. She is one of the few artists to have sustained such a long and respected career, making her a brilliant role model for others to follow.

As Duckworth points out, the art of getting through hardships is knowing when to adjust, adapt, and pivot. Success doesn't come from talent alone—it requires the ability to change, grow, evolve, and stay committed to our core passion. Duckworth highlights perseverance and adaptation as keys to success. But what if we could go beyond mere resilience and actually benefit from adversity? This is where Nassim Nicholas Taleb's concept of antifragility comes in.

In his book *Antifragile: Things That Gain from Disorder* (2012), Taleb explores how we can thrive from uncertainty. In regards to change, he maintains that rather than just withstanding stress, we can grow stronger from it. In fact, he points out that certain people, systems, and ideas don't just survive uncertainty and adversity—they actually thrive and improve from it. This applies even in times of chaos, when the whole world seems to have spun off its axis.

Let's break down this idea of *Antifragile:*

- Fragile people and systems crack under pressure; they struggle to cope with setbacks and change is one of those stress triggers.

- A resilient person weathers the storm but remains unchanged, like the palm tree I mentioned earlier, bending in the wind.

- Antifragile people benefit from stress. They become stronger over time, with each setback building up their abilities to handle knockbacks.

How do we get to a point where we can emerge from change stronger and more aligned with our goals? For Taleb, this involves a strategy that balances low risk and calculated risk.

For instance, if you want to transition from a corporate job to becoming an entrepreneur, a fragile approach would be quitting impulsively, risking financial instability. A resilient person might endure a job they dislike without making a change. But an antifragile person would start preparing in advance—researching, refining their skills, and testing the waters before making the leap.

This is where the antifragile approach proves useful: while still in your present job, you start researching the business you want to launch. You refine your skills, adjust your strategy, and gain confidence in your expertise before fully transitioning to your new venture.

You will go through periods of uncertainty and often need to go beyond your comfort zone. That's all part of the process of change—adapting to new challenges through trial and error. One thing is for sure: those who embrace uncertainty and adapt to challenges become more creative, resourceful, and stronger in the long run.

The civil rights activist Harriet Tubman is a powerful example of antifragility. She didn't just endure immense hardship—she grew stronger and more effective because of it, turning adversity into a source of power. She thrived in a period of uncertainty, adapted to danger, and became an unstoppable force for freedom.

Born into slavery in Maryland in 1822, Harriet suffered a traumatic brain injury when she was just 13. She continued to be plagued by health issues such as epilepsy, narcolepsy, and chronic migraines for the rest of her life. But that didn't stop her from achieving great things. Instead, these hardships only strengthened her resilience and purpose. She escaped slavery in 1849 and committed herself to helping others, including orchestrating the escape of 300 enslaved people using the Underground Railroad.

At the time, the Underground Railroad was unpredictable. The routes changed frequently, informants were in abundance, and the slave catchers were always on the hunt. Tubman was successful because of her adaptability, often switching tactics, taking different paths, and using a range of disguises. In fact, she became a master strategist, risking her life over and over again. You could say her approach mirrored Taleb's barbell strategy: she took both low and high risks but was never caught as she continually refined her tactics and adjusted where necessary.

Armed with her fervent beliefs in freedom and equality, Harriet also worked as a nurse, cook, and spy for the Union Army during the Civil War. Dedicated to supporting the women's suffrage movement, she was a significant figure in the fight for civil rights and racial equality. Her resilience and adaptability make her a shining example of incredible courage and conviction in the turbulent history of the U.S.

What can we take away from figures like Roberta Flack and Harriet Tubman? That we can thrive not in spite of our struggles, but because of them. We can build something as we go through change if we are prepared to adapt, be flexible, and believe in our capabilities.

Ryan Holiday's *The Obstacle Is the Way* (2014) explores how we can use Stoic principles to turn adversity into opportunity. When we focus on adaptability and embrace obstacles as paths to growth, it is possible to overcome life's challenges. Neuroscience supports this idea, showing how our brains are wired for adaptability and resilience. Of course, we need to train them to face the challenges rather than try to avoid them.

Our brains are not fixed; they are capable of rewiring themselves. This process is known as *neuroplasticity*, allowing the brain to reorganize itself by creating new neural connections in response to experiences, learning, and challenges. *(Doidge, 2007)* When challenged, the neural pathways associated with problem-solving, emotional regulation, and resilience actually grow stronger. *(Davidson & Begley, 2012)* If Rachel, who we met earlier, had remained in a fear-based loop, her brain would reinforce avoidance behavior, keeping her stuck in her situation. The small steps she took helped to create new neural pathways in her brain that supported courage, adaptability, and resilience.

Sometimes, when under stress, rational thinking goes out of the window. This can happen when we find ourselves in challenging situations and seismic shifts in our regular lives. When the philosopher Marcus Aurelius advised people to see obstacles as opportunities, he was basically asking them to reframe their negative experiences—a technique backed by modern neuroscience (Beck, 2011). By reframing the narrative, Rachel was able to activate her prefrontal cortex—that's the part of the brain responsible for executive decisions—instead of allowing the amygdala to take over.

You see, we can actively change the way our brain responds to situations, allowing us to get through difficult times. And each small win is a dopamine hit, making us even more motivated and determined. By understanding this process, we can rewire our thinking, turning adversity into a tool for growth.

Let's take a look at some self-reflective prompts based on Stoicism and neuroscience that can help guide you through embracing change, overcoming adversity, and adapting to life's challenges:

Exercise 7: The Key Tenets of Stoicism

1. **Reflect on the following:**

   What Can I Control?

   - What current challenge in your life feels overwhelming?
   - What parts of this situation do you feel like you can control?
   - What parts do you feel are beyond your control?
   - How can you change your response and move forward?

2. **Now, consider this question:**

   Are Obstacles Opportunities?

   - Think back to a time in your life when you faced what seemed like an insurmountable obstacle.
   - What did you learn from it?

- How can you approach a current challenge and turn it into a learning experience?

- What strengths or skills might emerge if you face it head-on?

3. **Perception shapes our reality. Changing how we view obstacles can transform our experience:**

    ### Change Your Perception

    - When you face difficulties, how do you typically perceive the situation? As a threat, or as a chance to grow?

    - What thoughts or beliefs stop you from seeing this as an opportunity for growth?

    - Can you change your perspective, viewing difficulties as stepping stones rather than setbacks?

4. **Consider the following:**

    ### Take Small Steps

    - What small steps could you take today to begin tackling your current challenge?

    - Think about how small actions can shift your mindset from one of overwhelm to empowerment.

    - How can taking action help you build momentum and confidence?

5. Looking at past successes can provide valuable insight into your resilience:

    ### Reflect on Past Successes

    - Think back to a time in the past when you showed resilience in the face of adversity.

    - What gave you strength during that time?

    - How did you adapt to overcome the difficulties yet stay true to your long-term goals?

    - Can you bring some of the strategies into your current situation?

6. In addition:

    ### Persevere Through Uncertainty

    - When you face uncertainty, what is your typical response? Do you give up, stay stuck, or find ways to adapt?

    - How can you develop patience and perseverance when things feel out of control?

    - What does moving forward look like for you, even if you aren't sure of the outcome?

7. Once you've reflected on challenges, consider how adversity has fueled your growth:

    ### Grow from Adversity

    - Think of a recent failure or mistake.

- What lessons did you learn from it?

- How can you apply those lessons moving forward?

- How can your current challenge help you to grow?

8. **Finally:**

    Adapting to Change

    - How can you adapt to new ways of dealing with challenges?

    - What new strategies or perspectives will help you move past this difficulty?

    - How innovative can you be in dealing with your current situation?

9. **Reflect and move forward:**

    - Reflect on the last month, year, or decade. Think of the ways in which your resilience and adaptability helped you navigate challenges or changes.

    - Based on your experiences and insights, what one action can you take today to embrace change, overcome an obstacle, or adapt in a way that helps you grow stronger?

By using these prompts, you can reflect on the challenges you are facing today and find ways to approach them differently. Reflection helps you to keep growing and feel empowered when life seems unpredictable and uncertain.

Cultivating Resilience in Uncertainty

Life's curveballs come in many shapes and forms. No matter what you are going through now, be it a career change, personal loss, or an unexpected challenge, it's resilience that guides us through uncertainty. A job loss, a breakup, a trauma, a loss—all of these life events will try to break us, but resilience teaches us one thing: instead of resisting, to move with those changes.

Mindset is key here. As psychologist Martin Seligman (1991) explains in *Learned Optimism*, it's how we view what is happening that determines how we respond to adversity. If you develop an optimistic mindset, you are more likely to see setbacks as temporary and specific rather than permanent and overwhelming. Instead of thinking, 'Why me?' try, 'This is tough, but I'll get through it." Sometimes, it's as easy as that—reframing your way of talking and thinking. And believe me, this is a skill you can build on if you stay aware of your thoughts and internal narrative.

You may think that resilient people are mentally strong, and that's true to a large extent. But apart from a capacity to bounce back, resilient people are also emotionally intelligent and have an acute sense of self-awareness. When you recognize your emotions and understand where they are coming from, you can make better decisions. This nurtures resilience over time, as you learn to pause, assess, and choose a response that serves you better.

Resilience isn't just about endurance. It's about knowing when to adjust, when to push forward, and when to pause. Think of it as a well-tuned violin. It's not just the strength of the strings that matters but also the sensitivity of the musician's ear. They can detect the slightest change in tone and know exactly when to adjust their bow. In moments of tension, the musician will adjust, pause, and find the harmony needed to create something beautiful. In the same way, resilience involves having self awareness and emotional intelligence to create harmony in your life. It's this fine balance between strength and sensitivity that makes all the difference.

If you are wondering how to build your resilience so that you can get through difficult changes and transitions in your life, there are several options.

You can try mindfulness, which can be practiced anywhere, any time. It really is a game-changer when it comes to resilience, since focusing on the present instead of worrying about the future helps to reduce stress and anxiety. Jon Kabat-Zinn's *Wherever You Go, There You Are* (1994) is a beautiful, practical guide to mindfulness, showing that resilience starts in the mind. One of the most inspiring quotes in the book is, "*You can't stop the waves, but you can learn to surf.*" In essence, while we can't control life's challenges (the "waves"), we can develop the ability to navigate and adapt to them with a calm, focused mindset.

If this resonates with you, simply take three deep breaths the next time you feel overwhelmed and focus on the present. Then, ask yourself, "What can I control right now?"

No doubt, there have been times when you felt alone in your struggles, or disconnected from others. Maybe you wanted to withdraw from everything, or focus on trying to work things out alone. I can understand that, although research shows that resilience is deeply connected to the relationships we enjoy and the support we receive, whether that be from friends, family, or mentors.

In *Option B: Facing Adversity, Building Resilience, and Finding Joy* (2017), Sheryl Sandberg and Adam Grant explore the idea of resilience after Sandberg suddenly lost her husband. One of the most powerful lessons she shares is that resilience strengthens when we lean on others. They can help get us through the hard times, so we emerge stronger and able to thrive, no matter what we have experienced.

As I said in the beginning of this chapter, change equals uncertainty and fear of the unknown. Instead of harboring such fears and assuming the worst, why not adopt curiosity about what is happening? This is the growth mindset I've also touched on, which is so important. When we can see one door closing as an opportunity for another to open, this takes away a lot of the fear.

With that in mind, how about reframing your thinking? Instead of saying, *"What if everything goes wrong?"* ask yourself, *"What could go right?"*

Key takeaway:

As we close this chapter, I want you to remember that, in most cases, change isn't something to be feared. On the contrary: it can be a powerful catalyst for growth and an opportunity to rediscover yourself or learn something new. When you adopt an open mind, change can build resilience. It reveals strengths you weren't aware of and brings new opportunities.

If you are experiencing some tumultuous change in your life, try to shift your perspective, seeing it as something that is happening *for* you, not *to* you. I know this isn't as easy as it sounds, but it is possible, believe me.

Welcome in the uncertainty that change brings because even in our hardest moments, we can find meaning and purpose. And try to live more in the present, focusing on what you *can* control now. With each small step, imagine how far you are able to go, with each action building new possibilities for you. And don't forget to surround yourself with a good support network–you don't have to go it alone all the time. Change can be a lonely road and is much easier to navigate when you have company along the way.

Each minute, hour, day, month, and year promises incredible growth. All you have to do is be flexible, adaptable, and keep moving forward. So here's the question: What is one small step you can take today?

CHAPTER 7

COMPARISON KILLS

"You don't have to prove anything to anyone. You just have to show up and be yourself."
—Maria Shriver

When was the last time you got caught up in numbers? Likes, shares, followers—chasing trends and influencers. Right now, the latest obsession is the pursuit of the so-called "perfect body," fueled by GLP-1 medications, airbrushed photos, and endless comparisons.

But real self-worth isn't measured in stats or social media validation, nor is it about finding someone—or something—to blame. It's not only about algorithms, fad diets, or the medical community's role in the side effects of our choices. True self-worth runs deeper. It's about understanding the journey that led us here in the first place.

What small, daily decisions contributed to the extra weight we now feel pressured to lose? Why do we keep choosing relationships that chip away at our confidence and well-being? Exploring these questions can open the door to greater self-compassion and a more honest, lasting sense of self-worth.

In reality, comparison pulls us outward, forcing us to seek validation from others, but integrity calls us inward to stay true to our values. We can only experience real change when we stop measuring ourselves against external standards and start facing our own truths with honesty, self-respect, and courage. Beneath the layers of expectation, conditioning, and comparison, who is the real you?

Are you the person your environment has shaped? Are you the version of yourself that developed in response to family dynamics, abuse, abandonment, or rejection? Have you lived your whole life trying to live up to a false ideal of who you should be? Although all of these experiences may have molded you, they don't define you. Deep within, your authentic self is waiting to be set free but you need to peel back the layers to discover it.

It's time to shift from simply surviving to undergoing a transformation that will reveal the person you were always meant to be.... the real you. Let's get to work on that!

The Trap of Constant Comparison

It's human nature to measure ourselves against others—we've been doing it since time began. Our minds are still wired to ask: *Am I strong enough? Smart enough? Do I fit in?*

In the past, this instinct was a survival skill that helped us navigate social hierarchies and find our place in the world. But today, in the age of endless comparison, it has morphed into something far more insidious. We've become fixated on how others look, what they are doing, and how successful they are. This obsession, when taken to the extreme, can quietly chip away at our confidence and well-being, making us feel somehow lesser or not good enough.

The need to compare starts at a very early age. From childhood, where we are taught to measure ourselves against others' performances—whether in school, their grades, achievements, or even their appearance. Society has a way of subtly reinforcing this by linking success with external validation and public approval rather than with personal fulfillment or integrity.

If, for instance, you love reading about history and know more than the syllabus requires but struggle in a test environment, you might feel like a failure. Meanwhile, your best friend crams for exams and memorizes the facts without understanding them. When they get straight A's, the system deems them "successful," even if their knowledge is short-lived. Society sees grades, awards, and recognition as superior to internal growth, curiosity, and mastery.

It doesn't mean we have to be opposed to healthy competition, but there's a significant difference between gaining recognition through true merit and celebrating hollow achievements. When we look at the perfect bodies, curated lifestyles, and so-called "success" stories around us, it's easy to fall into the trap of thinking these individuals are somehow "better" than us.

Some may argue that comparing ourselves to others can push us toward self-improvement, and that's true to a certain extent. But it can also lead to self-doubt, envy, discontentment, and unhappiness. No matter how much you want to look like one of the Kardashians, the reality is that you'll probably never get close—and even if you do, how does that truly increase your sense of self-worth?

For those of you who use social media a lot, it's important to be aware that what you see isn't always reality. The edited, filtered images on platforms like Instagram may look great but they give a false view of life. The negative effects on young women in particular who browse such platforms for several hours of the day has already been noted. A 2018 study by Fardouly et al. found that just 10 minutes of browsing Instagram increased body dissatisfaction in women between the ages of 18 and 25. If you look long enough at images of 'idealized' beauty or the 'perfect body type', it's sure to make you feel like your own body is not matching up to these ideals. That's where low self-esteem begins to fester, along with anxiety and even depression.

Another study by Tiggemann and Slater (2019) backed up these findings, suggesting that social media use leads to "higher levels of body dissatisfaction and lower body appreciation in both adolescents and young adults." In simple terms, the more time we spend on platforms like Instagram, the more likely we are to feel unhappy with our appearance.

While most of the research done so far has focused on younger populations, other studies show that adults also face pressure from curated content. For example, a systematic review found that social media use among adults is linked to changes in self-esteem, anxiety, and even depression. Another study revealed that frequent social media users report feeling more irritable, which suggests it's taking a toll on emotional well-being. So while we often talk about how these platforms shape youngsters, it's clear that we adults are also feeling the impact.

Taking this into account, it makes sense to be more mindful of how much social media we consume. The less exposed we are to excessively edited content, the less negativity we're likely to feel about our own appearance and self-worth. But it's not just social media that can create low self-esteem. In his book *The Paradox of Choice* (2004), Barry Schwartz argues that, in a world overflowing with options, we often become paralyzed, overwhelmed, and dissatisfied. We tend to focus on what we lack instead of our personal growth and achievements and this triggers our insecurities.

Decision paralysis, which Schwartz talks about in his book, is real and puts us in a constant state of dissatisfaction. How many times have you walked into a shoe store, only to find yourself overwhelmed by the variety of styles—sneakers, heels, sandals, pumps, and everything in between? Rather than enjoying the abundance of options, do you find yourself fixating on whether you're making the "best" choice? The question, "Do I look good in these?" has become a loaded one today, as we're not just asking about our appearance. We are really asking, "Do I match up to what's considered acceptable?" In other words, will I get the external validation I need to feel good about myself?

With so many options at our fingertips, it's easy to lose sight of what 'we' truly want. When we find ourselves in this constant state of indecision, our sense of inadequacy is only magnified, and that prevents us from experiencing genuine satisfaction and contentment.

In *The Happiness Hypothesis (2006)*, Jonathan Haidt explains how the world has gotten a lot larger over the past few decades. Once, we tried to measure up to our friends, neighbors, or colleagues. Today, we are pitting ourselves against people we will never meet from all over the globe. When our source of reference is so expansive, how can we feel enough compared to celebrities, influencers, and their airbrushed lifestyles?

This pressure to keep up seeps into every aspect of life—career paths, relationships, parenting, and even personal values. We are told what success *should* look like, with little compassion out there for anyone who fails to meet such unrealistic expectations.

First, we've got the "hustle" culture, which glorifies non-stop productivity over rest. Then, there's the wellness industry, which bombards us with unrealistic beauty standards. Let's not forget the model of the "perfect" family, career, or social life we see online and in the media, making us doubt our own choices. It's easy to lose sight of our deepest values in such a curated world.

The story of Phyllis Hyman serves as a poignant reminder of the danger of succumbing to external pressures and losing sight of our inner truths. A brilliant and talented artist, Phyllis had the world at her feet from the 1970s until the early 1990s, gaining significant attention early as a backup singer before launching her solo career in the late '70s and '80s. Her peak years were in the 1980s, with hits like *You Know How to Love Me* (1979) and *Living All Alone* (1986).

In 1995, she was preparing for an epic comeback at the Apollo Theater in New York City when, just days before her 46th birthday, she tragically passed away from a drug overdose. A note found by her side read: *"I'm tired. I'm tired. Those of you that I love, you know who you are. May God bless you."*

Despite being adored by her fans and peers, Phyllis struggled with mental health issues, including bipolar disorder, and found herself overwhelmed by external pressures that demanded more of her than she was able to give. The entertainment industry, in particular, often valued her in ways that did not honor her authentic self. Forced to perform for the sake of record sales and image rather than for her creative passion, she fell victim to the same pressures many of us face today—overindulging in food, sex, and anger as a way to fill the void left by years of not honoring her true self.

She wasn't alone in this. Many artists and public figures are expected to fit into molds that satisfy someone else's expectations and, much like us, the more they conform, the further they stray from their own sense of identity. The difference is that their struggles are often played out in the public eye, and Phyllis Hyman's tragic ending illustrates the devastating impact of these forces on mental and emotional well-being.

How often have you doubted yourself or questioned something that once felt right, simply because someone else is doing things differently? Quite honestly, this second-guessing can be exhausting, and the more we let external pressures shape us, the further we drift away from our authentic selves.

I call this self-betrayal because each time we silence our own desires, values, or instincts to meet external expectations, we are eroding our authenticity. Whether that's chasing a career we hate, pushing our bodies toward unattainable beauty standards, or trying to gain the approval of others, we are trading our souls. What's more important: doing what truly fulfills us or looking good from the outside? The more we get swept away with external ideals, the harder it becomes to recognize what truly makes us happy. We forget to stop and ask ourselves: *Do I even want this?*

There is a way to break free from this endless cycle and it begins with self-awareness. Instead of automatically measuring your worth by someone else's ideals, take a step back and reflect:

- *Are my decisions based on my values or out of a need to fit in?*
- *If outside opinions didn't exist, would my choices be the same?*
- *What does success, happiness, and fulfillment mean to me, on my own terms?*

I'm not suggesting that you reject ambition, beauty, or achievement, but that you make sure your goals are truly yours, and not just a response to outside pressure.

This isn't easy by any means and it requires confidence, self-reflection, and the courage to go against the grain. As Brené Brown said in *The Gifts of Imperfection* (2022), "True self-worth isn't something we earn through achievements or social recognition; rather, it comes from embracing authenticity."

What does that mean in practice? Well, for one thing, it's about owning our flaws, insecurities, and struggles instead of trying to hide or "fix" them. It means accepting that being imperfect doesn't make us inadequate—it makes us human. This idea of living in alignment with who we really are is a tonic for the soul. It frees us of those external demands to be someone else and allows us to enjoy life on our own terms, warts and all.

Staying True to Your Values Amid External Pressures

The path to staying true to our authentic selves lies in integrity. This is when we make sure our actions, choices, and values are in sync, regardless of what anyone else around us is doing. Failing to do so is like trying to fill a bottomless glass with water–it will never be full.

When we say *yes* to things that don't feel right, pursue goals simply to impress others, and edit our lives to avoid external judgment, we are compromising our sense of integrity. On the other hand, when we trust in our decisions, live by our values, and aren't afraid to go against the grain, we are choosing authenticity over approval, even when it's uncomfortable.

Stephen Covey talked about this in *The 7 Habits of Highly Effective People (1989)*. What's so transformative about the book is that it focuses on personal growth and effectiveness, with integrity being a key element. Covey emphasizes that true effectiveness and success come from living in accordance with timeless, universal principles, not from chasing momentary approval or recognition from others.

And we are all responsible for our choices and reactions, which set the foundations for living with integrity. Instead of making decisions based on what society expects of us, we are much better served basing our decisions on our principles. This beats any fleeting approval for external voices. The fact is that integrity isn't some abstract moral concept talked about in philosophical circles: it's a practical strategy for living a life of fulfillment.

Integrity demands that we are honest with ourselves, first and foremost. But how can we do that in a world where we feel the constant pressure to conform? Cultivating integrity into daily life is key to adopting new ways of being–ways that make us feel whole, authentic, and worthy in our own right.

Let's take a look at how to achieve this:

1. Check in with Yourself Regularly

Take a time-out to check in with yourself at least once a day. Turn off the autopilot and slow down to ask: *Am I doing X, Y, or Z because it aligns with my values—or because I feel pressured to?* This could relate to work, health goals, or even how you interact in personal relationships.

If, for example, you are trying to climb that corporate ladder and have become a 'yes' person in order to do so, how does that align with your self-worth? All of those hours working late, sacrificing your social life or time with family, may not be worth it in the long run. You see, chasing after what we think is 'expected' of us doesn't always lead to a happy end. We might just wake up one day with burnout, or realize our career isn't fulfilling us at all. When we stop to ask ourselves what we really want, we might discover we have been trying to live up to someone else's definition of success.

The same goes for relationships. How many people do you know who stay in a relationship not because they are happy, but because they feel they should? Perhaps you currently find yourself in that situation. When your gut feeling is telling you that something is missing but don't want to let others down, that is self-betrayal. It takes courage to own up to these truths but honoring them is worth much more than trying to meet the expectations of others.

2. Set Boundaries: Learn to Say No When it Doesn't Serve You

Kindness is one thing, but people-pleasing at the expense of your own well-being is another form of self-betrayal. Acting with integrity means honoring your limits, even if that disappoints or inconveniences others. It's important to cultivate the art of knowing when you agree to do something out of a sense of obligation or from a genuine willingness, which is why boundaries are so useful.

Think about the times you've said *yes* when you really meant *no*. How often have you agreed to plans you had no energy for, or squashed your feelings to avoid conflict? Each time you did so, you may have spared someone else discomfort, but at what cost? Living with integrity means practicing self-awareness and having the courage to look after your own emotional and mental well-being, even if it means letting others down occasionally.

If you have ever dreaded attending family gatherings because of the toxic dynamic but kept going because you felt *obligated*, you will know exactly what I mean. Although it isn't the easiest of things to do and you can expect some backlash, setting boundaries can actually create healthier relationships in the long run. When you only engage in relationships that feel healthy, it is possible to find more peace and confidence in your choices. I know that saying *no* can be hard, but it's often the only weapon you have in your armory to protect your well-being. Such a simple word, but so powerful!

3. Own Your Imperfections: Confidence Comes from Authenticity, Not Perfection

Do you believe that you need to "fix" yourself to be worthy? Do you feel the pressure to change your appearance, have a more successful career, get a bigger house, or think you have to be perfect? How would you feel about showing up for who you are–no filters, no apologies?

Self-acceptance is the foundation of genuine confidence. When you stop chasing perfection and embrace your flaws, quirks, and vulnerabilities, you give yourself permission to be fully human—to be fully you.

Think about the people you admire most in life. I am 100% certain that it's not their perfection that draws you in, but their authenticity. When you spend time with someone who can laugh at themselves, admit to mistakes, or stand firm in who they are, that's inspiring. Sure, we all have our strengths and weaknesses, but our uniqueness is worth so much more than we imagine. Instead of getting caught up in the vicious cycle of self-criticism and comparison, wouldn't it be lovely just to show up as your authentic self, no strings attached?

Consider what experiences, strengths, and perspectives you bring to the table that no one else can, and ask yourself:

- If I stopped worrying about what others think, how would I show up differently in my life?

- What are the parts of myself that I've been hiding or apologizing for?

- How can I practice self-acceptance today, in big or small ways?

- The story of self-worth starts with *you* and you don't need to change a thing to deserve it.

4. Define Success on Your Own Terms

The world is constantly telling us what success should look like—money, status, recognition. Everywhere you turn, some version of "making it" hits us in the face: the flashy cars, the Instagram-perfect lifestyles, the endless awards. But here's the thing: real success is deeply personal. It has nothing to do with what seems cool or desirable to others. It's certainly not about how many followers, fans, or likes you have. Real success is when you live your life in a way that is meaningful to you.

What does that meaningful life look like? Only you know the answer to that but you can consider what you value, what inspires you, what makes you feel alive!

Martin Seligman, a positive psychology expert, talks about this in his book *Flourish* (2011). He makes the point that true success isn't about chasing money or status. It's about living a life where you feel fulfilled, connected, and aligned with your own values. There's a good reason why he calls it "flourishing", because the more you feel good about yourself, the more you will thrive. It's not important how others see you, although if you can inspire them along the way, that's an added bonus.

So, the next time you find yourself measuring success by what others have or do, stop to ask yourself:

- What really makes me feel accomplished, even if no one else notices?

- What does success mean to me, on my own terms?

- What does a meaningful, fulfilling life look like for me, and not for anyone else?

When you make choices that align with your values, and live in a way that feels authentic, you will discover the true definition of success.

Building Integrity and Celebrating Your Unique Path

How can you escape the comparison cycle and begin to live a life of personal integrity? You can start by asking three simple questions the next time you feel inadequate in relation to others:

- Is this comparison motivating me or making me feel worse?

- Why am I comparing my reality to someone else's curated 5 second reel?

- Would I feel differently if I didn't have access to this information?

By asking these questions, you can help yourself to break the automatic comparison loop that drags you down into self-doubt. As soon as you become aware of how you truly feel, you can begin to shift your mindset.

Do yourself a big favor: take a break from social media or, at least reduce the amount of time you spend on it. Once you do so, you will start to regain perspective. More importantly, be selective about what you do on social media platforms and who you follow. Weed out anyone or anything that lures you into the comparison trap or makes you feel lesser about yourself. Instead, create a garden full of inspiring people who have achieved something worthwhile and fill your feed with positive stories. This may sound like a simple step, but it can be surprisingly transformative.

Another powerful tool that will level up your feel-good hormones is practicing gratitude. More than just thinking happy thoughts, gratitude helps you to appreciate what you have in life instead of feeling dissatisfied. Studies have shown that people who keep a daily gratitude journal experience higher levels of life satisfaction and lower levels of stress (Emmons & McCullough, 2003). For example, if you're feeling envious of someone else's financial success, write down three things you're grateful for today—whether it's the sunshine, a new opportunity, or simply your health. You can do this at any time of the day and I usually express my gratitude for three things in my life just before I go to bed each night. I find it helps me to sleep better, and I also wake up with a sense of contentment and calm.

Counting your blessings really can help you to appreciate everything you have in life and stop you from feeling unfulfilled or inadequate.

It takes courage to go your own way and risk the chance of being disliked. This is the topic of a great book by Ichiro Kishimi and Fumitake Koga, titled: *The Courage to be Disliked (2018)*, which is based on the idea that we shouldn't base our self-worth and happiness on the approval of others. Instead, we should take steps to live authentically and in line with our own values, even if others don't endorse what we do.

Imagine how liberating it can be to break free from the need for external validation and challenge conventional notions that say your worth is determined by how much others like or accept you. When you reach that mindset, you will be encouraged to make decisions based on what aligns with your own sense of purpose and integrity.

Exercise 8: The need for approval

Identify where you may be seeking approval from others and how to make decisions based on your own values:

Reflect on External Validation

- Identify areas where you seek approval from others (e.g., career, appearance, relationships).
- Consider how seeking approval affects your self-worth and happiness.

Identify Your Core Values

- Write down your top 3 core values (e.g., honesty, creativity, independence).

Scenario Practice

- Think of a recent situation where you were torn between authenticity and seeking approval.
- How would your decision change if based on your core values instead of others' opinions?

Take Action

- Make one decision in the next 24 hours based on your values, not others' approval.

Comparison Kills

Reflection

- After making your decision, reflect on how it felt. Did it bring freedom or challenge you to step out of your comfort zone?

A remarkable example of someone we have all heard of who acted with integrity and in alignment with his core values is Mahatma Gandhi. The leader of India's non-violent independence movement against British colonial rule was the embodiment of someone who had the courage to be disliked for the sake of his principles. His commitment to non-violence, truth, and social justice made him a thorn in the side of the British authorities, and although he faced widespread opposition, Gandhi refused to compromise. He was even prepared to face imprisonment for his beliefs, which came about after the famous Salt March. Totally opposed to seeking personal gain or power, he chose instead to live a very simple life that reflected his values.

Disliked by both British rulers, who saw him as a threat to their control, and some Indian leaders, who believed aggression was the only path to independence, Gandhi remained steadfast despite wrongful attacks. He endured imprisonment, criticism, and even violence, yet never wavered from his principles. He wasn't interested in approval or public adoration, but his actions changed the course of history. Through his leadership in India's independence movement, he proved that colonial rule could be overthrown peacefully, a revolutionary idea that reshaped political resistance worldwide.

Gandhi's approach to peaceful resistance later inspired political leaders such as Martin Luther King, Jr., who used nonviolence in the American civil rights movement, and Nelson Mandela, who fought against apartheid in South Africa. Gandhi's influence extended beyond politics, shaping modern movements for human rights, freedom, and social justice across the world.

His life highlights how acting with integrity can inspire others, even unintentionally. His famous words, "You must be the change you wish to see in the world," are a timeless reminder of the power of personal integrity, regardless of external validation or criticism.

You don't have to be Ghandi and want to change the world. Just be yourself and change *your* world, whether people like it or not!

Key takeaway:

We make comparisons all the time but the problem arises when our sense of self-worth is diminished when we don't feel good enough as we are.

Today, we aren't just comparing ourselves to a small circle of friends or acquaintances; the whole thing has gone global! Now we are face-to-face with complete strangers who are pushing their ideas of perfection, beauty, and success. It's no wonder, then, that this constant comparison leaves us feeling anxious, inadequate, and disconnected from who we really are. As we dwell with integrity and stay true to our values, we can stop chasing other people's versions of success and focus on what actually matters to us.

It's up to us to break the cycle of seeking external validation and get real with ourselves. It comes down to this: do our actions align with our values and reflect who we truly are? When we take a step back from social media, practice gratitude, and redefine what success means to us, we can break free from those unhealthy external expectations. Owning our imperfections and defining and redefining (when necessary) success on our terms helps us to cultivate real self-worth and fulfillment.

Remember, true fulfillment comes from living your own life with authenticity and integrity. So, let go of the need to be perfect and stop comparing yourself to unreal ideals or standards. As Brené Brown wisely says, "Owning our story and loving ourselves through that process is the bravest thing that we'll ever do." When you discover the power within to be unapologetically you, you'll discover a life far more fulfilling than any comparison could offer.

Celebrate your own successes. Enjoy your unique achievements. Respect your inner values and nurture greater well-being. Ask yourself: 'Am I living in alignment with who I truly am?' When you can answer 'yes,' that's all that matters.

CHAPTER 8

CUTTING THROUGH THE NOISE

"Within you, there is a stillness and a sanctuary to which you can retreat at any time and be yourself."
— Hermann Hesse

It's difficult to find focus in a noisy world. Today, distractions come at us from all sides and in countless ways, making us feel scattered, anxious, and disconnected. From the constant buzzing of our phones to 'urgent' notifications, it's natural to wonder why we just can't seem to pay attention to one damn thing. This pressure to keep up with everything is exhausting, giving us brain fog and a loss of clarity.

How often do you find yourself unable to focus, sitting down to complete a task but ending up spending half an hour going down a rabbit hole of wasted time? You are not alone. I even know many people who seem addicted to the constant noise, 'watching' a movie on their favorite streaming service while doom scrolling until they lose both the plot and their energy.

But you know what's worse than wasting time through external distractions? Losing your sense of self control and feeling unproductive, which ultimately leads you to question your worth.

Identifying and Minimizing Distractions

How do distractions do this? Very easily: by making us feel guilty for not being productive enough. This is known as the productivity guilt loop and it looks something like this:

You begin with a clear plan for the day, perhaps an important task or project to work on. Before you start, you check your emails, and one message leads to another. Sooner than you realize, you're responding to texts, skimming social media, and watching random YouTube shorts. An hour passes and you haven't made any progress on your main task, and that's the cue for frustration to set in. What do you say to yourself at that point? I *should* have been more disciplined. I've wasted half the morning. This cycle of productivity guilt can diminish your self-worth if repeated often enough because you start equating your value with your ability (or inability) to "get things done." It's easy to see why you would feel like you are failing, even though the problem isn't your inability to complete the task—it's the lack of attention management.

Whenever we get distracted, we are being pulled further away from a state of deep focus and closer to the state of cognitive fragmentation. This is when our mental processes are broken down into smaller, less cohesive parts, making it harder for us to focus, think deeply, or retain information. In his book *Deep Work (2016)*, Cal Newport talks about how modern distractions, especially from digital technology, contribute to the fragmentation of our attention.

While multitasking was once seen as a great skill to have, it now appears that frequent task-switching reduces our ability to perform deep, focused work. In truth, our brains aren't built for multitasking, despite what we've come to believe. Research suggests that the average person gets distracted every 40 seconds when working on a computer and it can take up to 29 minutes to regain full focus. Productivity expert Chris Bailey points out that our attention is one of our most valuable resources, yet we often squander it without realizing it (2018). What we need is for our brain to function in a state of "deep work" to perform at our highest cognitive level, and this means no distractions!

How many times have you sat down to watch a movie but pause every few scenes to check your phone? You've probably noticed that the story no longer flows, and you start to have gaps in the plotline. When you do this throughout the day, shifting constantly from one thing to another, how can you ever engage fully in anything?

Apart from draining our mental energy, neuroscientists have found that this kind of behavior also leads to decision fatigue, where even the smallest of choices seem overwhelming (Baumeister et al., 1998). And the more mental fatigue we experience, the more our confidence fails and we start to second-guess our abilities and decisions. The reality is that our brains can only handle so many decisions before they become "tired" and start making suboptimal choices.

Reclaiming focus isn't just about being more productive. It's also linked to how we treat ourselves. Whenever we allow distractions to dictate our days, we're reinforcing the idea that our time and energy aren't valuable. Once we take control of our attention, we send ourselves a different message that says: *I am capable of deep, meaningful work. I am in control of my own mind.*

It's this feeling of being in control that aids our self-confidence and inspires us to trust ourselves again. It gets us out of the productivity guilt loop and reminds us we are worthy of our own focus and attention.

How do we fight back against distractions? There are several ways, once we understand what is really going on in our brains. Neuroscience tells us that we can ignore distractions when we learn how to tune them out rather than simply try to focus harder. In this process, alpha brain waves help suppress distractions and keep us locked into the task at hand. But these waves won't work to the full when we are constantly switching tasks or glancing at our phones every few minutes. So, what we do really affects our internal state, even when we aren't aware of it.

The Impact of Technology on Focus and Self-Worth

When it comes to phones, there are some simple changes we can make to how we use them, such as turning off notifications or using apps that block social media. Cal Newport talks about Digital minimalism–removing non-essential technology so we can reclaim our ability to think deeply and create. As we all know, that's easier said than done when our devices are designed to keep us hooked. But it isn't just that phones distract us. We also need to recognize how technology shapes our attention and, ultimately, our self-worth. When we constantly lose focus, we aren't just fighting time management—there's another war of attrition going on under the surface–the feeling that we aren't living up to our own expectations. As we berate ourselves for not being good enough, or efficient enough, guess who makes an appearance? Procrastination!

Since distractions make it harder for us to focus, we often choose the path of least resistance, tending to easier tasks rather than getting to grips with the harder ones. This is structured procrastination, which is an avoidance technique that often comes with serious setbacks. Deciding to check our emails instead of knuckling down to a big project is the easy option, but the feeling of not accomplishing the most important task we had to do can leave a bitter taste in our mouths. We fall behind, miss our targets, and may even feel like a total failure.

Then, there's the dopamine trap–the one that lures us in with instant gratification. Responding to messages, watching a quick video–all of these actions give us a 'brain ping'; a dopamine hit. In our 2-minute culture, we value speed and efficiency above all else: we want it all now! From fast food and fast fashion to 'shorts' and 'reels', everything has to be instant and bite-sized. We are so used to getting quick rewards that we have almost forgotten what it is to be patient, since that requires too much effort.

On the other hand, deep work requires delayed gratification, which is hard to strive for when we are so accustomed to getting a quick fix. It can lead to frustration because it requires sustained effort—something we have gotten out of the habit of exercising. Procrastination then becomes even more tempting. Who would choose delayed gratification over immediate satisfaction? Why is it, for example, that many of us find it so hard to read a novel from beginning to end but have no problem with short messages? Could it be that we don't even make the effort anymore?

This is central to the problem of distraction, because real fulfillment doesn't come from quick fixes. It emerges from sustained effort and growth. The challenge we face is learning how to resist the pull of instant rewards in favor of something more meaningful. In effect, we need to retrain our brains to tolerate delayed gratification without feeling frustrated. That's where intentional boundaries with technology and habit-building strategies come in.

Instead of being in a reactive state, feeling the urge to respond to messages, and always on the edge for that next dopamine hit, we need to be more present and engaged. Reacting to the constant external stimuli means we aren't consciously choosing how we spend our time. We feel distracted, with no control over our lives and, eventually, lose confidence in our abilities to achieve anything of value. In contrast, completing deep, focused work gives us a great sense of achievement and reinforces our self-trust. It's the difference between running a 100-meter sprint and a 40 kilometer marathon—one needs that fast burst of energy, while the other requires pace, stamina, and persistence.

Staying the course and completing deep, focused work lets us see that we are capable of anything, leading to increased self-validation and personal growth.

Exercise 9: How distracted are you?

I want you to think about your relationship with distractions, instant gratification, and self-worth, by reading the following prompts:

1. **Understanding Your Distractions**

   What distractions pull you away from meaningful work most often?

   How do you feel after spending an hour on social media and endless scrolling?

   What situations or emotions make you more likely to seek these distractions?

2. **Exploring Instant vs. Delayed Gratification**

   When was the last time that you chose instant gratification, only to feel regret or frustration afterward?

   Can you think of a time when you resisted a distraction and felt proud afterward?

   How do you feel when you engage in deep work, as opposed to quick, surface-level tasks?

3. **Assessing the Impact on Self-Worth**

   Do you believe your productivity is linked to your sense of self-worth? Why or why not?

   How confident do you feel in yourself when you lose focus or procrastinate?

   What do you tell yourself when you allow distractions to take control of your time?

Cutting Through the Noise

4. **Setting Intentional Boundaries**

   What would the ideal work environment look like to you if it were free of distractions?

   What one change could you make today to reduce a major distraction in your life?

   How can you remind yourself that your focus and time are valuable?

5. **Building a Sustainable Focus Habit**

   How can you practice delayed gratification in your daily life?

   How can you make deep work more enjoyable or rewarding?

   How can you commit to a long-term goal or project with focus and patience?

These prompts should help you to identify your patterns, recognize the deeper impact of distractions, and help you to take meaningful steps toward focus and self-worth.

Now that you have had the chance to think about what habits and patterns you want to change, let's consider some practical steps you can take to retrain your brain and move from instant distractions to delayed gratification:

1. Kick the Dopamine Habit

- Turn off any non-essential notifications on your phone. If it isn't urgent, you don't need to respond to every ping. You can use apps like Freedom or Forest to block distractions.

- Delete any distracting apps that crave your attention or remove them from your screen. Hide them in a folder instead, which you need a password to access.

- Take a break from your phone, setting designated times throughout your day as fasting periods. Hang a 'Do Not Disturb' sign in an obvious place near you and free yourself of over-stimulation.

2. Retrain Your Brain with Small Wins

- Apply the "10-minute rule" and resist the urge to check your phone for 10 minutes. You will soon find that the craving passes.

- Give yourself micro-challenges, such as committing to reading for ten minutes before you go to bed instead of checking your phone one last time. Gradually increase the duration as your focus improves.

- It's not just about the results—your effort counts too so celebrate each win. You can do it!

3. Rebuild Your Attention Span

- When you need to do some focused work, set yourself a timer for 25–45 minutes to do it in, then take a break. You should be able to increase the duration over time.

- Reading long-form content has become a chore for many, yet make it a goal and commit to reading one chapter of a book per day. You will soon master the art of enjoying a good read instead of a few comments on social media.

4. Make Instant Gratification Hard

- Turn off your phone altogether, or place it somewhere out of sight.

- Use website blockers like Freedom or Cold Turkey to limit distractions.

- Create a dedicated distraction-free space and set up a 'focus ritual', such as soothing music, herbal tea, or aromatic candles.

5. Redefine 'Effort' as Something Enjoyable

- Instead of thinking, *I have to work on this task,* shift to, *I get to focus on something meaningful.*

- Gamify your focus sessions by challenging yourself to stay focused for 30 minutes without getting distracted.

- Start telling yourself you are someone who values deep focus and doesn't like distractions.

Can you think of any more ways to remove distractions in your life?

Through small, intentional changes, you can retrain your brain to resist instant gratification and embrace meaningful work. And with practice, you will become more in control of your choices and experience greater fulfillment.

Your attention is one of the most valuable things you have. It shapes your thoughts, impacts your work, and, ultimately, affects your sense of self. You need to reclaim it if you have been lost in the brain fog of insta-hits and fast feeds. You do know that you are worthy of deep focus, meaningful work, and your own time, right? There will always be distractions out there but when you choose depth over distraction, you're actually choosing to invest in yourself.

When we set boundaries and intentional limits on what we are prepared to engage in, we are sending ourselves some powerful messages:

> *My time and attention are valuable.*
>
> *I can control my life and focus on the meaningful, not the trivial.*
>
> *I am worthy of uninterrupted time.*

Instead of passively consuming whatever comes our way, we can actively create our lives and rebuild trust in ourselves, one step at a time.

One of the most powerful ways to counteract distraction and digital overstimulation is by practicing mindfulness—the practice of intentionally focusing on the present moment without judgment. By grounding ourselves in the here and now, we cultivate awareness and regain control over our attention. When we are fully present, we regain focus. More than that, we remember that our worth isn't dictated by algorithms, notifications, or online validation.

Practicing Mindfulness to Maintain Clarity

Technology isn't the only thing demanding our undivided attention and time. In this era of constant flux, political shifts, economic uncertainty, and the growing urgency of climate change, everything we are exposed to can become a source of distraction in our daily lives. The world around us generates a lot of noise, pulling at our attention and taking up our mental space.

If you follow the news, you will be only too aware of all the distressing reports and non-stop headlines about environmental devastation, war, social upheaval, and political instability. This creates anxiety about the world, leaving us feeling overwhelmed and helpless. How can we focus on more meaningful things when we are deafened by the constant noise of instability, conflict, and terrible events going on around us? And it isn't simply physical noise: it's emotional and mental.

Issues that seem so much bigger than us can easily cause paralysis, anxiety and a sense of helplessness. Climate change, for example, is always making the headlines, whether it's to do with extreme weather conditions, natural catastrophes fuelled by global warming, or the uncertain future ahead of us.

As someone whose life was disrupted by the devastating wildfires that affected Los Angeles County in 2025, I know first-hand what it feels like to be at the mercy of mother nature. Caused by the strong Santa Ana winds, severe dry conditions, and now seemingly coupled with Southern California Edison (SCE) negligence, the wildfires had a devastating effect. Apart from their economic impact, the emotional and mental toll is just as damaging. Watching your home, neighborhood, or familiar landscapes going up in flames leaves a profound sense of loss and helplessness. And the trauma doesn't end when the flames are extinguished: heightened stress levels and the fear that another disaster could happen again have a serious effect on one's mental health.

There's also the collective grief to deal with: witnessing an environment transformed into ash, and the emotional weight of what has been lost. Communities that once felt stable can suddenly feel insecure and unsettled. When disasters like this are broadcast live all over the world, it also creates a global sense of dread and doom, even if viewers are thousands of miles away.

Political shifts happening around the globe can also make us feel like we need to stay glued to our screen in case we miss something that might affect our lives. But as we get caught up in the external world 24/7, it's easy to lose track of our own direction.

Of course we need to be aware of what is going on around us, in our community, and the wider world, but the problem is that we can become too distracted. The more we are pulled into what is happening, the easier it is to forget our own needs and priorities. The risk is that we become so absorbed by these issues that our well-being is ignored. We have to remember that we aren't defined by what is going on in far-flung regions and our worth isn't measured by every global crisis. The most important thing is to engage with the world when appropriate, but not forget we need inner peace to thrive and grow.

This could be as simple as watching fewer news reports, not getting involved in every conversation about the latest disaster, or resisting the urge to comment on every political debate. If we feel like we *must* stay on top of the latest issue, we need to consider what the emotional cost of that is to our well-being. This external noise can become very damaging if we over-expose ourselves to it, because the information we digest begins to define who we are and what we care about.

If you feel like you haven't done enough to prevent climate change or haven't supported the right cause, you may begin to lose your sense of self-worth. When you scroll through your social media feed and see images of burning forests, melting glaciers, and starving children, it is natural to want to help. But between work, family, and daily responsibilities, you may feel that your capacity to take meaningful action is limited. When you see people sharing petitions, attending protests, and showing off their latest sustainable lifestyle choices, it can start to feel like you aren't doing enough. Guilt may take over and, instead of being motivated to take action, paralysis sets in. Is your self-worth to be measured against what you do in response to every global crisis? That's a heavy burden to bear, isn't it?

Our value isn't dependent on constant action but on recognizing our limitations and doing what we can. In any case, we have already mentioned that worth isn't something to be earned—it's an internal process that we have to cultivate.

So, where does mindfulness fit into all of this?

Mindfulness isn't just as a tool for individual focus but it's also a way to reconnect with our values and sense of control. When everything surrounding us feels chaotic, mindfulness helps to filter through the noise and focus on what matters most to us in the moment. It's about training our brains to stay present in the middle of everyday life. It's about noticing where our attention is going and *choosing* whether to follow it.

When we practice mindfulness, we learn to observe the world's chaos without becoming consumed by it. We will still care about the important issues, but we can also set boundaries to protect our mental space. They help us to focus on what we can control—our actions, our thoughts, and our responses. This shift strengthens our sense of self-worth, because we begin to recognize that our value isn't dependent on being overwhelmed by the world's crises. It's found in the choices we make, how we engage with others, and how we prioritize our well-being.

Ultimately, we are all navigating a world that is filled with deafening distractions—both personal and global. Although it's important to stay informed and take action in ways that align with our values, we also have to remember to live a life that is grounded, focused, and intentional. We don't have to be pulled into every headline or crisis; we can choose how to respond according to what is most meaningful to us. We need to take care of our mental and emotional health so that we can engage in the world in all its craziness from a place of clarity and purpose.

As we let go of the pressure to be constantly switched "on," we begin to reassert control over our attention—and in doing so, we reconnect with a sense of self-worth that's rooted in who we are, not in how much we can take on.

Jon Kabat-Zinn, a pioneer in mindfulness-based stress reduction (MBSR), explains that mindfulness helps us *become aware* of these moments instead of getting pulled in automatically. It gives us that split-second pause to ask: *Do I really want to do this right now?*

That's all mindfulness really is. Noticing. Pausing. Choosing.

Let's look at how easy it is to incorporate mindfulness into your daily life:

- Before responding to a notification, take one deep breath. That moment of pause helps you decide if it's worth your time.

Before opening another tab or checking your phone, ask: 'Is this what I actually want to do?' Just that question can shift your focus.

- Before you change channels on the TV, stop and think. What content do you want to expose yourself to–positive images or negative ones? When you feel the pull of distraction, name it. Saying "I feel restless" or "I want a dopamine hit" creates awareness—and awareness gives you back control.

Our pace of life forces us to run when we would rather walk. We've no time to stop and smell the flowers in the race to be more productive and to achieve more. The pressure to *always be on*—whether that is online or available 24 hours a day has become a part of everyday life. In his book *Four Thousand Weeks (2021)*, Oliver Burkeman offers a different perspective and one that may resonate with you. He points out the finite nature of life and reminds us that productivity isn't about fitting more into each day; it's about making deliberate choices about what truly matters.

You see, when we're constantly *trying to do it all*—multitasking, juggling deadlines, and racing against the clock—we might 'think' we are being productive, but it's often the kind of spent energy that leaves us exhausted and unfulfilled.

Think back to the last time you worked through a full day without really stopping. Maybe you were multitasking, working, looking after children, answering emails, or checking your phone whenever it buzzed. By the time evening came, you probably felt like you had been busy all day long but hadn't accomplished anything meaningful. Being 'busy' all the time is exhausting and not really that productive. As you respond to every demand that comes your way, it's difficult to focus on what is truly important to you.

This *always-on* mentality eventually impacts our sense of self-worth, since, if we aren't constantly doing something, we won't get the external validation we need. We may be able to check off our to-do list, but that list never ends. There will always be more to do tomorrow, and the day after that, ad infinitum, so we can never truly feel *enough*.

What if, instead of rushing through our days, we gave ourselves permission to choose what really matters? Instead of feeling like we *have* to do everything, we could focus on fewer things but give them our full attention. And, what about cultivating the art of doing nothing at all?

In contrast to our modern obsession with productivity, how about embracing contemplation, stillness, and non-striving? In the classic Tao Te Ching, Lao Tzu introduces the concept of wu wei (无为), which translates to "non-action" or "effortless action." This doesn't literally mean doing nothing but is more about a way of moving through life while following it's natural flow instead of trying to force things. The thinking behind this kind of wisdom is that by embracing stillness and allowing things to unfold naturally, we actually achieve more. As Oscar Wilde said in *The Importance of Being Earnest*, *"To do nothing at all is the most difficult thing in the world, the most difficult and the most intellectual."* Although he was making a comment about the Victorian workaholism of the time, it applies equally well to today's modern world.

When we let go of this need to "always be on," we open a space up for clarity. And with clarity comes focus. Wouldn't you prefer to focus on what is truly important instead of being distracted all the time by meaningless information? If you manage to do so, I can assure you that you will perform at your best. It's kind of like decluttering your bedroom or closet—once you remove all the unnecessary items and create some order, you also gain a greater sense of control. This is your space and you are responsible for how you use it.

A profound shift occurs when we move from *doing* to *choosing*. When we create that space for focus, we can begin to validate ourselves again from within and the need for external validation diminishes.

Instead of creating a 'to-do' list, create a 'to be' list.

How do you want to show up for yourself today? Do you want to feel fulfilled, content, and self-assured or anxious, stressed, and incapable? When you *choose* how you want *'to be'* instead of deciding what *to do* next, you will begin to feel differently. Our value comes from simply being present, intentional, and focused on what truly matters to us. When we acknowledge our own boundaries, time, and choices, we find that we are enough—just as we are.

Mindfulness allows us to do this—to slow down and really ask ourselves, *What do I want to focus on? What is worthy of my attention right now?* When we pause before reacting to distractions, we reclaim our ability to make decisions that align with our authentic values and goals.

Once you master it, mindfulness allows you to realize that clarity doesn't come from doing more—quite the opposite. It comes from choosing to do what means the most to you and giving it your undivided attention. By embracing more intentional focus, you're creating space for your own sense of self-worth, one that isn't tied to a never-ending list of tasks. And in return, you gain the gift of time—time to reflect, create, and be present in a way that brings fulfillment.

Key takeaway:

We will always be surrounded by distractions from the outside world, whether it's the constant ping of our phones, the temptation of endless scrolling, the overwhelming demands on our daily lives, or the global chaos. What matters is the way we interact with that noise so we can take back control.

This begins with understanding how our brains work and why distractions feel so alluring. Social media, emails, and instant gratification trigger dopamine spikes, keeping us in a cycle of reactivity rather than intentional focus, However, once we become aware of these tendencies, we can learn new habits and learn to set boundaries that protect our attention.

By establishing healthy boundaries with technology, we can begin to regain clarity and create an environment that encourages deep work rather than constant multitasking. But these boundaries aren't enough in themselves; we also need to strengthen the ability to be present.

Mindfulness helps us to do so, by noticing when our attention drifts and gently guiding it back to what truly matters. Instead of reacting, we can practice pausing, taking a deep breath, and checking in with ourselves. It's amazing how a single moment of awareness can change everything. We can move from being passive consumers of distraction to active participants in our own lives. Over time, mindfulness helps us to improve focus and strengthens our self-worth, reminding us that we are in control of how we spend our most valuable resource—our attention.

Next time you catch yourself reaching for your phone or drifting off mid-task, stop. Pause. Breathe. Ask yourself—where do I want my attention to be? The answer to that question can change everything!

CHAPTER 9

STRENGTH IN SUPPORT

"Connection is why we're here; it is what gives purpose and meaning to our lives."
— Brené Brown

We all want to feel connected. It's a deeply ingrained human trait to seek out the warmth of a touch, a familiar face, and the feeling that we belong. This need has its rewards when met, since social bonds do wonders for our emotional and physical health. We are naturally designed to thrive in relationships, not just survive in isolation.

Anyone who's seen the movie *Cast Away* (2000), starring Tom Hanks, will recall how Chuck (Hanks) is stranded alone on a deserted island after a plane crash. Forced to survive through hunger, illness, and injury, he also faces extreme loneliness. In his desperation, he turns a battered volleyball into a friend, naming it Wilson. What Chuck craves—what we all would in that situation—is an emotional anchor to help us endure isolation.

It's easy to understand Chuck's need for connection. As human beings, we're wired for relationships. Research shows that having strong social bonds not only boosts our sense of self-worth but also makes us more resilient and content (Holt-Lunstad et al., 2015). When we know someone has our back and supports us through tough times, life feels a little easier. Yet, in today's world, many are finding these connections are fading, leaving them feeling adrift and alone, much like Chuck in the movie.

We seem to be experiencing a loneliness epidemic, one that was amplified by the seismic shift in how we relate to each other during the COVID-19 pandemic. Personal contact and face-to-face communication were replaced by social distancing, Zoom calls, and a growing sense of detachment or isolation. Even after restrictions were lifted, many people struggled to reconnect, both physically and mentally, to the old ways of close contact.

Never before in history have we seen such a phenomenon on a worldwide scale. Billions of people were forced to adhere to social distancing measures over a period of repeated lockdowns lasting two years or more, making long-term social isolation a reality for many. While technology kept us digitally connected, research now shows that this often exacerbated feelings of loneliness, anxiety, and depression.

In 2023, U.S. Surgeon General Vivek Murthy declared loneliness a public health crisis, emphasizing its serious impact. He also noted that nearly half of American adults had reported feeling lonely even before the pandemic began. For those already struggling with loneliness, the lockdowns only heightened that sense of isolation. Our daily routines were dramatically altered—remote work, closed schools, and limited social interactions made many feel cut off from the world. As a result, mental health issues spiked, particularly anxiety and depression, with young adults and the elderly being hit hardest.

The World Health Organization (WHO) reported a 25% increase in anxiety and depression disorders worldwide after the pandemic (WHO, 2022). What's even more alarming is that social isolation has been shown to be as harmful as smoking 15 cigarettes a day, contributing to heart disease, stroke, and dementia (Holt-Lunstad et al., 2010). It's truly terrifying to think about the impact of loneliness on our health, and that's why we must prioritize building strong support systems.

This chapter is dedicated to ensuring that no one walks through life unsupported. By building strong, authentic relationships, we can nourish our sense of belonging and self-worth.

The Importance of Healthy Relationships

Why exactly are strong support systems essential for our self-worth? And why do our social connections have such a profound impact on how we feel about ourselves? Some researchers point to self-compassion as the cornerstone of mental well-being (Neff, 2011). From this perspective, self-compassion—being kind and understanding toward ourselves—is deeply connected to the support we receive from others. When we practice self-compassion, we're much more likely to reach out for help, which can prevent us from sinking into despair.

But beyond just asking for help, social connection reminds us of something fundamental: struggle is a shared human experience. Everyone faces challenges, setbacks, and moments of doubt. Knowing this can counter feelings of isolation and loneliness. Additionally, when we feel connected to others, we're less likely to be harsh on ourselves, silencing that negative inner critic.

Think of it this way: if you're struggling emotionally, your instinct might be to withdraw, telling yourself that no one could possibly understand what you're going through. This reaction creates a cycle—self-isolation feeds negative emotions, making you feel even worse. But if you have the courage to reach out to trusted people, you'll receive emotional support and a renewed perspective.

The truth is that having the right connections helps us realize that we aren't alone in our struggles. When we allow ourselves to be vulnerable within a safe circle, it opens the door to growth, resilience, and a deeper sense of self-worth.

In this disconnected world, it's easy to feel alone. The less authentic contact we have with others, the greater our sense of isolation, and that can have devastating consequences. This is reflected in the rise in suicide rates. According to the Centers for Disease Control and Prevention (CDC), suicide rates in the U.S. increased by 2.6% in 2022 alone. Tragically, suicide is now one of the leading causes of death among young people worldwide. This represents an extremely worrying mental health crisis, and though the reasons behind it are complex, at its core, it's about struggles with isolation and hopelessness. Many people simply feel unseen, unheard, cut off, and alone.

Yes, we can all be 'digitally' connected, but that's an illusion. We may be 'plugged in,' online, and have hundreds of 'friends,' but none of that can compensate for genuine connection. Instead, we often feel disconnected—surrounded by people we have no real relationship with—people we never see in person or even speak to. This lack of authentic human contact can leave us feeling empty, unseen, undervalued, and devoid of any sense of belonging. That's why meaningful support systems are so important. And if we are struggling with anxiety, depression, or any other kind of mental health disorder, having a strong network to support us becomes even more essential.

We may find ourselves surrounded by many people yet still not feel seen. A tragic example of this is that of actor and comedian Robin Williams. His brilliant talent and amazing energy made him one of the most beloved figures in entertainment, bringing joy and laughter to millions. But behind the public persona was a man suffering from severe depression and anxiety, as well as a neurodegenerative disease called Lewy body dementia. This illness, which affects cognition, mood, and perception (Jellinger, 2023) wasn't well known at the time of Williams' death, although it's now clear that it significantly worsened his mental health. Unfortunately, he eventually took his own life.

Williams' tragic end reminds us that mental health issues are often invisible, silent, and can go unnoticed—even for someone in the public spotlight. As the late actor once said, "The worst thing in life is to end up with people that make you feel all alone." His story is not unique. How many times have we all felt alone, isolated, and in need of someone to talk to? And how many people have been lost to suicide because they felt there was no one there to catch them when they fell?

That's why we need to start cultivating deep, meaningful connections and ensure we surround ourselves with people who will uplift us, rather than deplete us. We also need to learn to recognize when someone in our circle is struggling and be ready to show up for them. In a world where loneliness is an epidemic, building and maintaining a strong support system isn't just a luxury—it's a life-saver.

You might connect with many people during a regular day through various mediums and interact with hundreds over your lifetime, but most of those interactions won't result in genuine connections. Your tribe—your close circle—may not add up to more than a handful of people. The key is that they are the ones who truly see, understand, and support you. If you're still looking for your tribe and struggling to build those crucial connections, it's time to take action. No one deserves to feel alone.

What do we mean when we talk about 'tribes'? Seth Godin, a marketing expert and thought leader, describes them well as "*small, tight-knit communities bound by a shared purpose, passion, or belief*" (Godin, 2008). This isn't just about marketing strategies—it's about our mental and emotional well-being. Our tribe members are the ones who inspire us, make us feel good about ourselves, offer unconditional support, and see us for who we truly are. They celebrate our successes, stand by us in our darkest times, and lift us up when we fall.

But we need to build our tribe with intention—not everyone deserves a place in it. Old friends, acquaintances, family members, or colleagues may be around you, but that doesn't automatically make them part of your tribe. I can't stress enough how important it is to surround yourself with the right people—those you choose to connect with in meaningful ways.

This might mean letting go of superficial relationships with people who don't bring value to your life and ending connections that are toxic or harmful to your mental and emotional health.

In my own journey, one of the hardest truths I've had to accept is how trust often has to evolve with time and experience. For years, I believed that if I gave enough, loved enough, and cared enough, I could change the dynamic of relationships where I felt taken for granted. I thought if I made enough deposits into people's lives, I would eventually be valued in return. But that was an illusion. What I learned is that where I plant is not always where I harvest, and sometimes, the soil I've chosen isn't the right one for my growth.

The hardest part about that realization wasn't the disappointment or the betrayal—it was the future wishing. I had projected more onto those relationships than they were ever able or willing to give back. And that broke me. But it was also where my resilience began. I had to learn to trust not just in others, but in myself; to trust that I would be okay even if I had been let down.

Trusting myself to make better choices, to grow through the pain, and to let go of the parts of me that kept seeking validation from the wrong places has been a painful but powerful part of my transformation. I'm learning that my worth doesn't depend on others' actions but on the faith I have in myself and the ability to move forward, even when the trust I had in others is shaken.

Perhaps you have gone through similar experiences and are still navigating the murky waters of toxicity, looking for a lifeline to grab onto. It might require swimming a little harder, but know this: once you learn to recognize who truly has your best interests at heart, you'll find the strength to keep going.

Recognizing and Releasing Toxic Connections

What exactly is a toxic relationship? That's a great question. You may know people who leave you feeling drained, unheard, or diminished. They are the ones who are hurtful, self-absorbed, or mysteriously absent when you need them most. If you interact too often with such individuals—be they friends, family, or colleagues—they can gradually make you feel emotionally exhausted and full of self-doubt.

Think of the boiling frog example: if you throw a frog into boiling water, it will immediately jump out, right? But if you place it in tepid water and gradually turn up the heat, the poor frog won't realize until it's too late that it's being boiled alive.

It's the same with toxic relationships: the harmful effects seep in slowly, until you find yourself feeling worn down. If someone constantly undermines you, uses emotional manipulation, tries to make you feel guilty, or only reaches out when they need something from you, your confidence and well-being are at risk. What might start with minor criticisms, subtle attacks on your opinions, or negative comments disguised as jokes can eventually make you feel worthless, inept, and emotionally drained.

As Dr. Naomi Eisenberger, a social neuroscientist, found in one of her studies on healthy relationships, social rejection activates the same brain regions as physical pain (Eisenberger, 2012). In other words, unhealthy relationships—whether emotionally neglectful, manipulative, or outright toxic—aren't just harmful emotionally; they are biologically damaging.

What are the red flags to watch for when trying to recognize if your relationship with someone is toxic? They may include behaviors such as:

- **Lack of empathy:** Perhaps you know someone who constantly dismisses or minimizes your feelings.

- **One-sided support:** If you feel like you are always the one giving but never receiving, this one-sided dynamic is unhealthy.

- **Emotional manipulation:** If a friend, colleague, or family member tries to make you feel guilty, gaslights you, or tries to control your behavior, that's emotional manipulation.

There are other signs to watch out for, too. Toxic relationships can manifest in many forms, and you may not initially identify them as such. It could be that you know the person so well that you just assume that's how they are and don't question whether their behavior is doing you harm.

For example, they may frequently put you down, mock your ideas, or make you feel inadequate. Over time, this persistent negativity can erode your self-confidence, as constant criticism is extremely toxic.

Maybe this person has unpredictable mood swings, forcing you to walk on eggshells around them. Feeling anxious about how someone will react if you say 'the wrong thing' is a major warning sign that your relationship is unhealthy.

Equally concerning is when the person fails to support or celebrate your successes and is always trying to one-up you instead. That's not the sign of a true friendship; your relationship shouldn't be based on unhealthy rivalry.

Another red flag is when someone rarely takes responsibility for their actions and always blames others for their mistakes. These individuals refuse to apologize and make excuses for their hurtful behavior.

Then, there are boundary violations—whether physical, emotional, or related to your personal space. This kind of invasive behavior shows little or no respect for your privacy and individuality, serving as a clear indicator of an unhealthy dynamic.

Toxic relationships also often involve attempts to isolate you from family or friends. If someone tries to discourage you from seeing loved ones or subtly undermines your other connections, that's controlling behavior and is definitely not healthy or acceptable.

Finally, if you feel that you can't trust someone or rely on them because they've lied and let you down repeatedly, that's a huge red flag you can't ignore.

When your relationships consistently leave you feeling drained instead of supported, it's time to set boundaries—or even walk away altogether. You have the power to choose to cultivate strong support systems in your life, rather than maintaining relationships that harm you. It's not easy, but once you begin to cut toxic ties and replace them with healthy bonds, you'll feel the difference.

If you are surrounded by people who genuinely have your best interests at heart, they will lift you up—not tear you down. Psychologist Dr. Marisa Franco outlines the key elements of a strong support network in her book *Platonic: How the Science of Attachment Can Help You Make—and Keep—Friends* (2022). She identifies three crucial factors:

1. **Mutual Trust & Emotional Safety.** Feeling seen, heard, and understood without fear of judgment.

2. **Reciprocity.** Enjoying a healthy, balanced relationship where both sides are willing to give and take.

3. **Emotional Availability.** Having connections who show up consistently, especially when things are tough.

These three elements form the foundation of deep, meaningful relationships. When we cultivate them, we don't just feel better emotionally—we thrive. Research has shown that strong social bonds like these can lower stress, improve resilience, and even increase life expectancy (Holt-Lunstad, 2017). Ultimately, building the right support network is about more than just personal happiness; it's about creating a healthier, more fulfilling life that's sustainable in the long run.

Despite what you might think, letting go of toxic relationships doesn't necessarily mean cutting off contact completely (unless it's necessary for your own safety). Often, it's better to shift the dynamics gradually—this could mean limiting the time you spend with certain people or distancing yourself emotionally from those who consistently bring you down.

Approach this process with self-compassion. Remember, you are doing what's best for you. You may feel guilty at first or worry about stepping away from someone, but your first priority is maintaining your values and self-esteem. The goal isn't to hurt anyone intentionally; it's about acknowledging your needs and choosing relationships that provide genuine support rather than emotional exhaustion.

Letting go of toxic relationships can be difficult, especially if you've known the person for a long time. It's important to remember that your well-being takes precedence. Staying in a relationship out of obligation or fear is unhealthy, and you have every right to build connections that uplift you, not weigh you down. When you surround yourself with people who affirm your worth, you'll begin to realize that choosing healthy relationships isn't selfish—it's absolutely necessary.

It's equally important to invest in the people who bring out the best in you, make you feel emotionally safe, and nurture trust. This is a two-way street—you can't expect to earn these things if you aren't putting in the same energy and effort. To help you reflect on your relationships and take action toward building a strong support system, consider these three key questions:

1. Are the relationships in your life helping your well-being, or doing you harm?

2. Are you committed to finding and nurturing your tribe?

3. Are you willing to be vulnerable and open to build deeper, more meaningful connections?

Depending on how you answer, these questions can guide you toward relationships that truly serve you, even if it means stepping out of your comfort zone for a while. When your circle of friends or family members isn't supportive enough, you'll lack the stability that a strong support system can offer. This is especially important if you're battling internal

Strength in Support

struggles like depression, loneliness, or poor mental health. While you desperately need to be understood by the people around you, things can go wrong very quickly if no one has your back.

We only need to look at celebrities in the public eye to see how devastating it can be when there's no trusted tribe to lean on. One example that stands out is Kanye West, the Grammy-award-winning artist, entrepreneur, and cultural icon. Considered by many to be a musical genius, his rise to fame has been shadowed by his public struggles with bipolar disorder. While his talent brought him global recognition, his lack of stable, grounding relationships has cost him dearly. His public outbursts, erratic behavior, and controversial social media posts have frequently led to ridicule rather than understanding. Instead of being surrounded by people offering consistent, compassionate support, he has often found himself in the company of enablers, critics, or fair-weather friends.

This is a dangerous place for anyone to be. Without that solid foundation of trusted relationships, mental health challenges can easily spiral out of control. We all need genuine, stable support. For celebrities, though, their struggles are played out for the world to watch, which can be devastating. Kanye's experience shows us how vulnerable we are to emotional instability, self-doubt, and even self-destruction when we lack meaningful, reciprocal relationships.

Having a solid support system cushions us against the hard punches life throws our way. Imagine being a boxer in the ring, but with no ropes to catch you when you're thrown backward—you'd struggle to stay in the fight, let alone win the round. It's the same with relationships: your tribe is like those ropes, helping you bounce back and keep going. True friends and mentors offer perspective when emotions become overwhelming, call you out when you're heading down the wrong path, and listen without judgment when you simply need to be heard.

And just like a boxer who trusts the ropes to keep them steady, having the right people in your corner can mean the difference between staying down and rising stronger than before. This applies to everyone, whether in the public eye or simply navigating the ups and downs of everyday life.

Creating a Supportive Network for Growth

You know the saying, "You are the average of the five people you spend the most time with"? It's true when you think about it, as our relationships shape who we are, how we feel about ourselves, and how we navigate the world. In essence, the people around us have a massive influence on our mental well-being. That's why it's crucial to surround ourselves with the 'right' people—the ones who empower us and help us thrive.

In his book *Give and Take* (2013), Adam Grant explores the dynamics of relationships and how they impact success. According to Grant, people tend to fall into three categories: takers, matchers, and givers. The secret to building a strong, empowering network is to surround yourself with givers—those who support, uplift, and help without expecting anything in return.

Grant argues that givers often enjoy the greatest success because they forge relationships based on generosity, collaboration, and mutual respect. Relationships with givers create an environment where support flows freely in both directions, with help being given and received.

But how do you cultivate these kinds of relationships in a world where social media and the workplace often reward the opposite? A good strategy is to begin paying attention to how you feel when interacting with someone. Does the conversation leave you feeling energized and supported, or drained and unheard?

You may know plenty of people in your life who are simply enablers—they support you, but not in a way that's beneficial to your well-being. Consider, for example, a so-called friend who says yes to everything you do, never challenges you to be better, keeps you in your comfort zone, and feeds into your negative habits without pulling you away from toxic situations. They may 'appear' to be supporting you, but in reality, they're stopping you from growing into the best version of yourself.

On the flip side, true friends will hold you accountable and offer constructive criticism when needed. When such friends are honest with you yet support you through your struggles, they are the ones to hang onto.

At this point, you might be thinking, "OK, that sounds reasonable, but how do I find these 'healthy' relationships?" One way is to seek out mentors—people who believe in you and are willing to invest in your success. As Sheryl Sandberg notes in her book *Lean In* (2013), mentorship is the key to both personal and professional growth. It's not just about receiving advice from some wise old sage or guru—it's more about establishing authentic relationships with those who have walked the path before you and can offer you the wealth of their experiences. A mentor can help you open up to new possibilities, take you beyond your fears, and encourage you to exceed your limitations, one step at a time.

Much in the same way that a tribe supports each other, having a mentor and a close-knit group of trusted friends can do wonders for your personal growth and self-esteem.

Another powerful way to build a strong support system is through the use of a feedback loop. This is the process of actively seeking feedback from those you trust, allowing them to offer perspective on your behaviors, actions, and emotions.

This loop enables you to grow while staying grounded. Asking for help when you need it— whether it's for emotional support, advice, or practical guidance—creates an ongoing cycle of mutual care. It's a reminder that we all need help at times, and asking for it doesn't make us weaker; it makes us stronger.

A feedback loop also strengthens relationships by keeping communication channels open and creating a safe space for honesty, vulnerability, and emotional support. Being open about your struggles and needs becomes easier when you know you're in a supportive environment, one where deep connections can be formed.

This means being intentional about who you connect with and the communities you choose to engage with. Many online groups and forums can offer valuable support, so it's worth engaging in those that truly add value to your life, rather than mindlessly scrolling through endless feeds that can leave you feeling more disconnected. Surrounding yourself with like-minded people, whether online or offline, helps you find the support you need.

In all your relationships, be mindful of who you spend time with and how those interactions make you feel.

Exercise 10: Building a Nurturing Support System

If you want to create a support system that nurtures rather than drains you, here are some actionable steps to consider:

1. **Recognize Negative Patterns**. Pay attention to how you feel after interactions with certain people. Do you consistently feel drained, anxious, or less confident after spending time with them? If so, it may be time to reassess that relationship.

2. **Identify Your Emotional Needs**. What kind of emotional support do you need? Are you seeking validation, empathy, or encouragement? Once you identify these needs, you can connect with people who are able to meet them.

3. **Start Small**. Begin by reaching out to people you already know to strengthen your connections. Small steps, like inviting a friend to coffee or lunch, or joining a group based on your interests, can be a great start.

4. **Be Vulnerable**. Share your struggles and allow others to open up about theirs. When we exchange experiences, we foster long-lasting bonds rooted in empathy and compassion.

5. **Set Boundaries**. Protect your emotional space by setting boundaries with people who drain your energy. Choose to cultivate relationships that nurture your personal growth and well-being.

You might be the type of person who hates asking for help—and I completely understand. I used to find it incredibly difficult to reach out to others, especially when I needed help the most. We all have our own stories, but more often than not, we're afraid of being seen as weak, incapable, or unable to solve our own problems. This fear of judgment can lead to even greater feelings of isolation, prompting us to build impenetrable barriers. But this isn't really living. We need to cultivate authentic relationships for our emotional well-being, and that means breaking the stigma of asking for help.

It's easy to fall into the trap of thinking everyone else is 'managing' while we're somehow failing. When we look at others seemingly sailing through life without any problems, there's a temptation to believe there's something wrong with us. The pressure to 'succeed,' to be 'happy,' or to do well is immense—especially when we're internally struggling just to keep it all together.

In her book *Radical Acceptance* (2003), Tara Brach highlights that true strength lies in vulnerability—being able to ask for help, and admit that we can't do everything alone. She talks about radical acceptance, which essentially means accepting ourselves as we are, without feeling shame or guilt about our need for support. It's this very vulnerability that allows us to form stronger, more meaningful connections, rather than shutting others out and isolating ourselves.

Now is a good time for you to reflect on how you feel about asking for help. Use the following prompts to get a clearer picture of how you cope with vulnerability and the potential benefits that come from it:

1. Think about a time when you hesitated to ask for help. What was holding you back? When you did finally reach out, how did you feel? If you didn't reach out, how did that affect the outcome?

2. Do you consider asking for help a strength or a weakness? If you view it as a weakness, what mindset shift can help change that perception?

3. How did the help of someone who supported you in the past strengthen your relationship? What did it feel like to receive that support?

4. Think back to when you've helped someone in a meaningful way. How did that impact your relationship with them?

5. When a friend or loved one asks you for help, how do you usually respond, and what emotions come up for you?

6. Are there any cultural or personal beliefs that influence your willingness to seek support? If so, do any of these beliefs need reframing?

7. What's your idea of a strong support system? How can you cultivate that in your life?

The main thing to remember here is that asking for help isn't a sign of weakness. It takes courage and self-awareness to reach out to others. When you do, you open the door to more meaningful connections and deeper relationships.

Still feeling uneasy about asking for help? Maybe you feel guilty, worrying that you'll be a burden or that you should be able to cope on your own. In *The Art of Asking* (2014), musician and artist Amanda Palmer shares how much of her career was spent learning to ask for help. Though she didn't feel comfortable at first, she eventually realized that by doing so, she was creating mutual, meaningful relationships.

Think about it for a second: when someone asks you for help, do you see them as weak? Probably not. You're more likely to appreciate the fact that they trust you. It's a two-way street. When you let people in and admit you're not superhuman, it actually strengthens your relationships. Give it a try!

As we come to the end of this chapter, I hope you have learned the importance of creating a supportive network. Remember that true strength lies in the connections we build with others and you don't need to do everything alone. Recognize when you need help, have the courage to ask for it, and nurture relationships that empower and uplift you. Embrace vulnerability, set boundaries, and surround yourself with your tribe–people who genuinely care about your personal growth and emotional well-being.

Key takeaway:

It's not easy to build a strong support system. Stories of public figures like Robin Williams and Kanye West show that success doesn't shield us from pain but, whether you're a celebrity or not, everyone needs to be surrounded by authentic connections.

Practicing self-kindness and compassion is essential too, which you can nurture by having a support network of trusted friends, mentors, and even accountability partners. Getting feedback will help keep you grounded, and also serve as a reminder that no one is alone in facing life's challenges.

You also need to have a willingness to be vulnerable. Asking for help may be one of the hardest things you have ever done, but it can also be one of the most empowering. Along the way, recognizing toxic relationships, setting boundaries, and letting go of harmful ties are all part of the growth process.

In the end, no matter where you are in your journey, you need others to flourish. Once you create a strong support system, you will be able to weather life's storms with greater resilience, knowing you are not alone. Remember that we humans are hard-wired to seek out connection so go out there and start building your tribe. When you have that bedrock in place, you can overcome any challenge!

CHAPTER 10

TRUE WEALTH

"Wealth is the ability to fully experience life."
— *Henry David Thoreau*

What pops into your head when you hear the word "wealth"? Do you immediately think of big bucks in your bank account, a garage filled with luxury cars, a sprawling house with a pool, or a jet-set lifestyle?

In today's capitalist society, we're sold the idea that money is the ultimate marker of success. The more you earn, the more important you must be. But this version of wealth is pretty one-dimensional. Sure, it can buy comfort and convenience, but there's no guarantee of happiness, peace of mind, or a sense of purpose.

We're constantly bombarded by messages that tell us to work harder to achieve more—more income, more recognition, more material stuff. In a world where success is measured by accumulation, it's no surprise that self-worth gets tangled up with net worth. So many people find themselves chasing money, thinking it's the secret to lasting joy, only to end up burned out and disillusioned.

On the hamster wheel of hustle, productivity, and performance, hardly anyone ever takes a step back to ask, "What does wealth really mean to me?"

There's also the underlying fear that if we're not achieving, earning, or climbing some invisible ladder, then we're falling behind. As the divide between the 'haves' and the 'have-nots' increases, nobody wants to belong to the latter side. But what if we've been looking at it all wrong? What if the real divide isn't about money at all, but about alignment? In other words, how connected are we to our values, joy, and well-being?

Take my friend Mike, for example. He had what many of us would call a dream job—a Product Manager at a large tech company, with an office to match his 6-figure salary, a luxury condo on the coast, and what appeared on the outside to be an exhilarating lifestyle. But on the inside, he was worn out, stressed, and running on empty. He had invested so much of his time and energy into his career that he had become estranged from his family, had never married, and his so-called friends were no more than business associates. When he finally decided to take a short sabbatical, he headed off on a surfing trip to the rugged coastline of Big Sur, a place he'd always wanted to visit but never made the time to do so. What he found there wasn't just swell and solitude, but something he didn't even know he'd been missing.

The ocean didn't care about Mike's status or deals. There were no deadlines, no pressure, and no demands on him there. As he paddled out on the first day, he rediscovered his passion for catching the waves and that thrill of riding them. He felt alive! When he made camp for the night with his one-man tent and the stars his only company, a question surfaced in his mind that he had been avoiding for years: *What is my life really worth?* The answer came to him in an instant. It's not the big office, the stock options, or the pats on the back. His worth was based on his time, his peace of mind, and on the people he loved and no longer saw.

That trip to Big Sur shifted something within Mike. He remembered how surfing had once been his first love, long before venture capital and IPOs. It took him back to a time when he felt genuinely happy and joyful, and he wanted to reclaim those feelings. Although he returned to his job after a few days and threw himself back into the corporate machine, he was unsettled—although it took another few months before he finally decided to quit. He reconnected with his family, caught up with old friends, and began a coaching service for young entrepreneurs. He still worked hard but was now diverting his energy to something that felt worthwhile, and he stopped measuring his worth by the size of his paycheck. Now, he spends a lot more time surfing!

As with most 'a-ha' moments, it doesn't mean that everything suddenly changes overnight, but they do create small windows of light that we can't ignore. One of the most illuminating realizations I hope you gain from this chapter is that self-worth doesn't have to be based on your finances. Instead of asking how much you have, it's a good time to consider a version of wealth that's based on your values, not just on value. Instead of asking how much you have, a better question might be, "Are you living a life that reflects what you truly care about?"

Shifting Perspectives on Financial Success

I'm always amused by the term "**High-Net-Worth Individuals.**" It's a stark comment on how society measures people, based on what they have. No one talks about "**High-Life-Worth Individuals,**" which makes much more sense to me. We all know that the financial models society is based on equate success with accumulation. But there is another perspective, one that measures wealth in terms of meaning and fulfillment.

Think about it: does financial wealth really matter if you're unhappy, isolated, disconnected, and misaligned with what's truly important to you? I'm sure your priorities are pretty much the same as most people's—to be healthy, to feel safe, to spend time with people you love, to have purpose, freedom, and peace of mind. These are the things that make life rich, but you won't find them on any balance sheet.

In their book *Your Money or Your Life* (2018), Vicki Robin and Joe Dominguez introduce the concept of "life energy." They invite us to reflect on how much of our time and vitality we're trading for money, and whether that exchange truly aligns with what we value most. At its core, financial freedom isn't necessarily about having more; it's often about needing less. When we feel content with what we have and stop chasing the next big thing, we free ourselves from that nagging sense of lack and the constant urge for more.

Our desire for something deeper isn't just something we wrestle with individually. We've seen this reflected in the choices of people who've decided that wealth can mean more than just money. People like Yvon Chouinard, the founder of the clothing line Patagonia, come to mind, who challenged the idea of what being a successful entrepreneur means.

Chouinard was a lifelong climber and environmentalist who built his very successful outdoor gear company with a deep respect for the planet. He stunned the business world in 2022 by announcing that he was giving the entire company away, transferring ownership to a trust and a nonprofit dedicated to fighting climate change. Rather than selling the company, which he felt would compromise its values, he announced that, "Earth is now our only shareholder." Chouinard wanted to leave a unique legacy behind him, one that showed true wealth wasn't measured by having billions in the bank, but in how that wealth is used for the greater good.

Your day-to-day life may feel miles away from the example of Patagonia, and you probably aren't in a position to give away millions of dollars. But the message behind the move is something we can all relate to. It is possible to align our resources with what we truly care about. Chouinard's story isn't just about philanthropy; it's about values. And that's something we can all reflect on. Whether talking about your time, money, or energy, the point is to live in accordance with what really matters to you.

True Wealth

But how do we bring that kind of clarity and alignment into our everyday lives, especially when we're juggling bills, careers, responsibilities, and economic uncertainty? Let's consider the points below:

Exercise 11: What does true wealth mean to you?

You can begin by asking yourself some simple questions:

- What does wealth really mean to me?

- When have I felt truly "rich" in my life that wasn't related to money?

- Am I using my time and energy in ways that align with what I most care about?

- What would "enough" look like for me, financially, emotionally, and for a lifestyle?

- Am I chasing more out of habit, pressure, or fear?

Once you reflect on these questions, you can try taking one or two small, practical steps:

- **Do a values check.** What are your top five personal values? Write them down, then look at your spending. Are they in sync?

- **Define your "enough."** Be specific about what 'enough' means to you. How much money, time, or stuff do you really need to feel content?

- **Reclaim your time.** Write down how you spend your time every day. Can you reduce the time spent doing activities that drain you and invest more time in doing what replenishes you?

- **Choose purpose over prestige.** When you next need to make a decision, ask yourself, "Does this align with the life I want, or the life I think I should want?"

- **Practice gratitude.** Each morning or last thing at night, name one thing that you are truly thankful for, whether that's your health, a child's smile, or the blue sky above.

I'm not suggesting that you ditch your ambitions or ignore the financial realities of your life. Money is a necessary evil in this world, and we all have bills to pay, goals to achieve, and things we want to enjoy. What I am suggesting is that you take a step back and realign yourself with what really matters. When you go from focusing on simply accumulating wealth to living a life based on your values and passions, this will change how rich you feel, no matter what your bank balance says.

You may end up living paycheck to paycheck for years, saving every penny for a bigger house or a fancier car. But does that define who you are and your real worth? A more fulfilling sense of wealth can come from within once you reconnect with your values and what is most important to you. If, for instance, you gain great satisfaction from spending time with your family or volunteering at your local soup kitchen, that's real wealth because you are fully engaged and acting with purpose.

When is "enough" ever enough? Ask some of the world's billionaires, and even they probably can't answer that. Imagine that you amass enough money to last you for several lifetimes—would that ever be enough for you? We only need to look at some of the richest individuals on the planet, such as Elon Musk and Jeff Bezos, to know that they are always in pursuit of more. More innovation, more influence, more power, more reach... it never ends. So, what is your "enough," and does that align with your values and your idea of self-worth?

Sure, the pursuit of "more" isn't just about money—it's about status, power, and validation. When we buy into the belief that the more money we have, the greater security, happiness, and contentment we will enjoy, we are going down the wrong track. No matter how much wealth we have, we will always want more if our self-esteem depends on it.

The need to constantly chase more isn't always about filling an empty space or achieving ultimate happiness. It's more about keeping up with the chase itself, as if the end goal isn't that important. Psychologists Daniel Kahneman and Angus Deaton looked at how money affects happiness and concluded that it does so only up to a point. They found that once people reach around the $75,000 a year mark, they don't feel any happier on a day-to-day basis. The fact is, while wealth offers comfort and security, it doesn't equate with happiness in the long run.

You could say that the more we chase money, the less likely we are to find lasting happiness. Unfortunately, we live in a society that makes us believe our self-worth is tied to external success. This belief goes against what Self-Determination Theory suggests. This theory, developed by psychologists Edward Deci and Richard Ryan, tells us that we're happiest when we make decisions that align with our true values, instead of just chasing external validation.

Research by psychologists Kasser and Ryan (1996) supports this idea. They found that when people focus too much on material success, they tend to experience more anxiety and feel less satisfied with their lives. In contrast, those who focus on personal growth, relationships, and well-being report higher levels of happiness and fulfillment. The takeaway here is that our well-being isn't necessarily about what we have, but about how we live and the choices we make based on what truly matters to us.

Have you ever set your sights on getting something new—a car, a boat, a house—and when you finally acquire it, it feels amazing? How long after attaining it did the novelty begin to wear off, leaving you feeling dissatisfied once again and in pursuit of something new? This is what's called the hedonic treadmill, a concept introduced by psychologist Philip Brickman. Basically, we often return to our baseline happiness level, no matter what we acquire. So getting that bigger house or nicer car doesn't lead to permanent happiness since the thrill wears off pretty soon.

The brain also has a part to play in this since it gets hooked on rewards that come from success. Each time we achieve a goal, the dopamine released makes us crave the next hit, the next milestone, the next achievement. This response is no different from what we might experience if we show addictive behavior, which could explain why we keep chasing more wealth, even if we are financially well-off. So, our drive to have more is hardwired into our brain and not easy to switch off. What we can do, though, is reframe our sense of what 'enough' means to us, and some ways to do this are through mindfulness and gratitude.

By giving thanks for what we have, we become more attuned to what really matters, instead of feeling the urge to chase external things that don't bring us true fulfillment. Mindfulness can also help us to break the cycle of constant craving by allowing us to appreciate the present moment. Through self-awareness and being in the "now," it's much easier for us to reconnect with our true sense of self-worth. It's almost like a veil is lifted as we see that our true worth lies in who we are and what we value.

In other words, instead of running after the next best thing, if we slow down and consider what is really important to us, that drive to fill a void will eventually fade away. We realize that everything we value is already here.

You may have heard of the term 'time-poor' being branded about these days. It's usually used in the context of busy professionals who don't have enough hours in the day to focus on certain things, such as meeting goals, spending time with family, or simply taking a break during their busy day. If we want to redefine wealth, we have to consider how we spend our time because this is one of the clearest indicators of where our wealth lies.

If, for instance, you're always rushing around trying to meet one obligation after the other, constantly chasing targets and trying to fit it all in, it's easy to get caught up in the "more is better" mentality. While we are told that time is money, what if it has more value than that? What if time itself is the truest form of wealth?

You have probably experienced that pressure to be "successful," and may have found it overwhelming. It's easy to understand why we get caught up in the illusion that financial success, recognition, and accolades are the ultimate measures of wealth. And yet, there is another way of defining success—one where we achieve inner calm, balance, and peace. In reality, we can't always control our financial situation, but we can control how much we focus on sufficiency rather than scarcity. This is one way to feel truly wealthy: when we feel full gratitude for the blessings we do have in our lives.

In *The Soul of Money* (2003), Lynne Twist argues that we don't live in a world of scarcity, but in one of sufficiency, if we can see it that way. As she mentions in her book, her time spent working with low-income communities around the world showed her that those with very little material wealth lived with a profound sense of generosity, gratitude, and abundance. Twist noted that their "sufficiency" wasn't about having less—it was about knowing what was enough.

This idea of redefining wealth and success is something Peter Diamandis is also passionate about. You might know him as the guy behind the XPRIZE Foundation—a global competition that offers multimillion-dollar prizes for tackling some of the world's toughest problems. From cleaning up our oceans to bringing education to underserved communities using AI, Diamandis is a tech entrepreneur turned philanthropist who also co-founded Singularity University, which helps leaders use fast-moving technologies to drive positive change.

Unlike other tech moguls, who are often in the headlines for their high-stakes ventures and disruptive ideologies, Diamandis focuses on collaboration, empowerment, and creating lasting, scalable solutions to the problems that affect us all. While Musk dreams of moving everyone to Mars, Diamandis asks how we can use innovation to improve life here on Earth. He puts it beautifully in his book, *Abundance*:

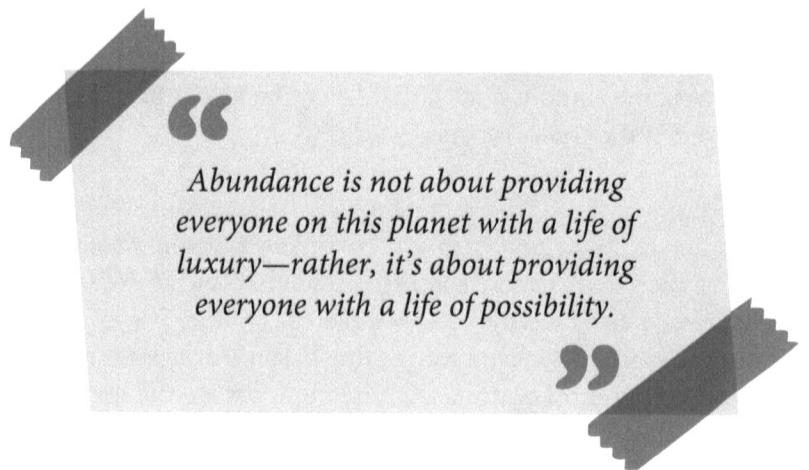

> *Abundance is not about providing everyone on this planet with a life of luxury—rather, it's about providing everyone with a life of possibility.*

Diamandis doesn't propose abundance as a nice idea or a feel-good buzzword. For him, it's a real, measurable shift toward greater access and opportunity for everyone. He is all about redefining wealth, not chasing markets to monopolize, and we can apply the same mindset in our personal lives.

Instead of seeing abundance in relation to income or status, we can see it in terms of meaningful work, time with our loved ones, and overall well-being. Just as Diamandis views technology as a way to unlock human potential, we can view our choices as tools to unlock personal abundance. Whether that means choosing work that aligns with our values, managing our time better, or doing more of what brings us joy, we can experience abundance every day.

The Connection Between Money and Self-Worth

Most of us are carrying around deeply ingrained beliefs about money that were often shaped in childhood. The way we earn, spend, save, and even talk (or avoid talking) about money are all influenced by these subconscious beliefs. Often, we make decisions based on such beliefs without even realizing it, and in ways that don't serve us.

Drs. Brad and Ted Klontz talk about these beliefs as "money scripts": what we pick up from family, culture, or early experiences (*Mind Over Money*). For example, if you grew up hearing things like "money doesn't grow on trees" or "rich people are greedy," you are more likely to associate wealth with guilt or shame—even when you work hard to achieve it. That is a surefire way to self-sabotage, such as expecting less money for your time spent working, undercharging for your services, or feeling uncomfortable when you achieve financial success.

If your parents struggled financially and you watched them struggle to make ends meet, you may have developed a **scarcity mindset**, where you feel anxious about spending money even when you're doing okay. In this case, perhaps you believe that you never have enough—whether it's time, money, or even love. The more you focus on what is lacking, the more stress you experience, no matter how much wealth you have accumulated.

Then, there are people with a **poverty mindset**, who have developed limiting beliefs and emotional patterns due to living in or near poverty for a long period of time. It's usually accompanied by feelings of helplessness, low self-worth, and the belief that success is out of reach. Anyone with such a mindset can fall into the trap of making decisions based on short-term survival instead of long-term growth, such as avoiding risks, resisting change, or believing they will never succeed. There's also the danger for someone growing up in a household where money isn't a problem to use it to self-soothe. Think of the people you know who overspend, impulse buy, or use money as a way to seek validation—and I think you get the idea.

The good news is that we can change these "money scripts" we play out in our heads and rewrite them. One of the best ways to do this is to look back at your financial story. To learn more about what kind of "blueprint" you are following, here are some prompts:

What Kind of Financial Blueprint Are You Following?

1. **Do you feel uncomfortable spending money, even when it's on something you need?**

    This could be a sign of a **scarcity mindset**. When you have enough, but it never feels like enough, and you tell yourself you should be saving more, doing more, or preparing for what could go wrong, this is a mindset rooted in fear. You may be afraid of instability or loss, and even abundance can be overshadowed by feelings of scarcity.

2. **Do you believe that wealth and success are for "other people"—not for you?**

    That's related to a **poverty mindset**, where you aren't just afraid, but you question your whole identity. You may tell yourself, "No matter what I do, I'll never get ahead. People like me are no good at the money game." Imagine how curtailed your life can become if you harbor this kind of mindset—you don't apply for better jobs, you dare not ask for a pay increase, and probably don't even allow yourself to dream big.

3. **Do you use spending as a way to feel good, in control, or validated?**

    Welcome to the **overspending mindset**, where money becomes emotional. For you, money isn't just a transaction—it's recognition of your worth, a reward, a way to feel you belong. If you spend money as a means to soothe stress, you will know only too well that the high wears off soon enough, leaving you feeling low again.

I want to point out that you shouldn't feel bad about these money scripts, whichever one you identify with. See them as outdated modes of thinking that no longer serve you. While they may have been useful in the past as a way to survive and adapt, they really don't have to define your future. As soon as you recognize the script, you can start to rewrite it and move from a mindset of fear and guilt to one that nurtures empowerment and self-worth.

Your self-worth has nothing to do with your net worth, and that's backed by research. In her book *Daring Greatly*, Brené Brown points out that money can be one of the biggest shame triggers we experience. When we have debt, suffer a job loss, or just don't feel "successful enough," the subject of money evokes deep feelings of inadequacy or fear. But Brown reminds us that vulnerability opens the door to real connection and healing. When we start being honest about the pressure we feel and admit to our insecurities, we can start to cross the bridge of shame. We aren't our salaries, and our bank balance doesn't define us either.

Our worth lies within us and it's who we are, not what we earn or accumulate. So how do we heal from money wounds?

It begins when we stop to ask, *Whose story am I living?*

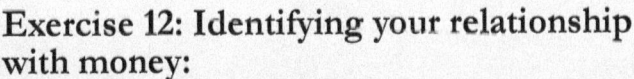

Exercise 12: Identifying your relationship with money:

Here are some prompts to help you start identifying and healing those money wounds:

- What is my earliest memory of money, and how did it affect what I believe today?

- What did I learn about money growing up, and have my perceptions changed at all?

- Does money make me feel safe, anxious, excited, or something else?

- How could I build a healthier relationship with money? (Example: seeking help with my finances, talking about my money worries, or simply acknowledging my fears.)

Let's now look at some prompts to get you on a healing path:

- What limiting beliefs about money can I leave behind?

- How can I go from believing "Money is scarce" to thinking "I am worthy of abundance"?

- What bad financial habits or patterns can I change, and what new habits can I replace them with?

Remember that healing isn't about suddenly becoming wealthy overnight or managing your expenses effectively. It's about being honest with yourself, practicing self-compassion, and building a healthier relationship with money. This involves moving away from the idea that you are what you earn or spend and focusing on who you are inside.

Creating Wealth That Aligns with Your Values

Forget the idea that your money, time, and resources are a measure of true wealth. It's not about investing in bitcoin or following the markets; neither is it related to material goods and possessions. Instead, it's about knowing what your deepest values are and making decisions based on them. But how do you define your values in the first place?

Think about what really matters to you and what you stand for. Rather than going along with the idea that success equates with how much money you have/have not and what 'things' you own, consider if all of this is really that important. What about living sustainably, caring for your loved ones, building a strong community, or supporting causes close to your heart?

Ask yourself: What do I really care about? Take a sheet of paper and write down what comes to mind, with some examples here to help you on your way:

- Family
- Health
- Generosity
- Sustainability
- Education
- Equality

After you've made your list, think about each one. Which values really reflect your innermost beliefs and resonate with your priorities? There are no right or wrong answers, but take the time to focus on what values from your list feel the most personal and meaningful.

Once you've identified your core values, think about how you can live in alignment with them every day. This means making intentional decisions that support your deepest priorities, such as spending more time with family instead of working so many hours. Perhaps you can donate some money to causes you support or take small steps to reduce your carbon footprint. Whatever lights you up, decide how you can spend more energy on that and less energy on activities that don't reflect your innermost values.

If you have savings and would like to use them in a way that reflects your values, socially responsible investing (SRI) or ESG investing can be the answer. These kinds of investment strategies focus on companies and funds that prioritize environmental sustainability, social responsibility, and ethical governance. It can be a great feeling to know your money is making a positive impact on the world—if you can spare it.

Some investing options in the U.S. that align money with meaning include ESG-Focused Mutual Funds & ETFs such as:

- **Vanguard ESG U.S. Stock ETF (ESGV)** A fund that avoids investing in companies involved in fossil fuels, firearms, and tobacco, focusing instead on firms with strong ESG practices.

- **iShares MSCI KLD 400 Social ETF (DSI)** This aids investors seeking large- and mid-cap U.S. companies with outstanding ESG ratings.

- **Parnassus Core Equity Fund (PRBLX)** Known for its strict screening, this fund excludes fossil fuels and invests in companies with a corporate culture based on fairness and promoting environmental sustainability.

You can also invest in your community through credit unions and community development financial institutions (CDFIs) such as:

- **Hope Credit Union** (Mississippi-based), which invests in historically underbanked communities across the Deep South.

- **Calvert Impact Capital**, which offers Community Investment Notes to fund affordable housing, clean energy, education, and small businesses, especially in marginalized communities.

There are online platforms you can check out to help you decide where to invest, depending on your pet cause or interests, such as:

- **Ellevest** Founded by Sallie Krawcheck, this investment platform focuses on women, offering ESG portfolios focused on social equity and sustainability.

- **OpenInvest** A platform you can customize to align your investments with causes you care about, like LGBTQ+ rights, climate change, racial justice, and more.

A good example of someone who's really using his wealth to live out his values is Robert F. Smith, the founder of Vista Equity Partners. The company focuses on software and tech company investments, but at the heart of it lies Smith's support for education and social justice for Black communities in the U.S.

Growing up in a working-class neighborhood in Denver, Smith was inspired by his parents, who both cared deeply about causes that uplifted underprivileged communities. His mother even took him to the historic Jobs and Freedom March in Washington in 1963, where Dr. Martin Luther King delivered his "I Have a Dream" speech. Over the decades, Smith recalls his mom sending off a $25 check to the United Negro College Fund (UNCF) every month, and it's experiences like these that shaped his belief that everyone can help to make the world a better and more equitable place.

In 2019, he put his money where his mouth is, paying off the student loans of the entire graduating class of Morehouse College, a historically Black men's college in Atlanta. He also created the Student Freedom Initiative program to help students at Historically Black Colleges and Universities (HBCUs) have access to higher education without taking on crushing debt. His vision of long-term empowerment is a reminder that when money is used with intention, it can do much more than it would sitting in someone's bank account.

Smith is solid proof that aligning your wealth with your values is truly transformative and, in his words, "We will all be measured by how much we contribute to the success of the people around us."

Investing with a purpose allows you to create a health-building strategy that reflects your core values, and that is a very empowering feeling. But if you don't have spare money to invest, you can also give your time and energy. Being generous with those two elements is one thing we all can do, whether that's helping a neighbor in need, giving away old clothes to charity, or taking a moment to call a loved one to ask how they are. When we focus on generosity as an 'asset,' our perspective on money will shift, bringing us into alignment with our values.

We can also start taking a good look at where our money goes and ask ourselves: "Does this purchase support my values or reflect the lifestyle I truly want to live?" Instead of buying goods from large supermarket chains, we can buy from local, sustainable businesses. Small shifts in habit can bring us closer to enjoying a lifestyle that reflects our core beliefs or donating a small percentage of your income to causes you believe in. We don't need to make drastic changes overnight. Even shifting a few habits here and there can help guide us toward a lifestyle that reflects our core beliefs.

In her memoir *Wild: From Lost to Found on the Pacific Crest Trail*, we learn of Cheryl Strayed's real-life drama about hitting rock bottom. After the death of her mother, a divorce, and a period of self-destructive behavior, Cheryl finds herself emotionally bankrupt. Looking for meaning in her disconnected world, where she has been used to seeking external validation, she decides to take the 1,000-mile hike alone along the Pacific Crest Trail.

During the course of her trek, she begins to let go of excess emotional baggage and the heavy internal narrative that told her she wasn't enough. The hike becomes a metaphor for reclaiming her self-worth by reconnecting with what is important to her. By the end of her journey, she finds something more valuable than material wealth–a sense of purpose, clarity, and inner peace. As she mentions in her book, "I didn't know where I was going until I got there."

We don't always know which direction to take in life or what the final destination is, but one thing is for sure: our journey is much 'richer' when we let go of learned beliefs about net worth and concentrate on our self-worth instead.

When we shift the conversation from net worth to self-worth, we stop chasing someone else's idea of success and start getting in touch with what really matters to us.

Create a Personal Wealth Manifesto

It's a great idea to create your own wealth manifesto—one that really speaks to your inner values. All it takes is for you to write a short paragraph about what wealth means to you today. There are no wrong answers. Simply open up to whatever resonates with your core being and speak your own truth.

You can start by completing the following prompts:

- To me, wealth means…
- I feel rich when…
- I feel most aligned with my values when I…
- My life is abundant because…

Place your manifesto on your fridge, add it to your journal, or keep it on your phone and revisit it whenever you want to reconnect with what really matters to you. Make your wealth manifesto your mantra and never forget–true wealth is about living life on your terms, in your own unique way.

Key takeaway:

I guess you have realized by now that true wealth isn't just about money. It's about living a life aligned with your deepest values and focusing on what truly matters to you. That sense of richness shifts from material possessions to purpose and fulfillment when it's aligned with the important things in life: family, friends, health, well-being, and values. Living in a way that feels authentic and meaningful can make us feel much richer than all the money in the world. So, rewrite your old money scripts and embrace a mindset of abundance to move away from fear and scarcity. Instead, embark on a life where you make choices that reflect your true self.

Self-worth isn't tied to financial status, and the sooner you let go of comparing yourself to others or chasing external validation, the easier it will be to reconnect with what matters most. By aligning your wealth, whether through investments or acts of generosity, with your personal values, you can create a life that feels both prosperous and fulfilling.

Take the time to define your own version of wealth, and live by that vision every day. It's the key to cultivating a life of abundance, no matter your financial situation.

PARTING WORDS

Now that we've come to the end of this book, I invite you to pause for a moment and reflect on the journey we've traveled together.

This hasn't been a tidy, linear path toward some ideal version of self. Instead, we've navigated the messy middles—the spaces between who you were and who you are becoming. And as you acknowledge this moment, I want to remind you of something deeply important: You are worthy.

You will have realized that this book isn't about offering you a quick fix or a simple crash course in self-esteem. It's about embodying a truth that you must live, practice, and remember. That's the beauty of your worth—in its quiet constancy, in those messy moments where doubts and questions try to overwhelm you. And yet, you remain standing tall. If you've ever doubted that you are 'enough,' here's my answer to you: You are enough, simply because you are.

Think back to where we began, reimagining worth. We started by shaking off society's pressures—those unrealistic expectations that your value is tied to perfection, flawless performances, and social approval. Together, we busted that myth wide open. Perfection is not the goal. What matters is embracing yourself, in all your imperfect, vulnerable glory.

We also examined how easy it is to lose sight of our worth by comparing ourselves to others or letting external judgments define us. But remember: true value often resides in the quiet, subtle ways we show up for ourselves and others, even when no one is watching. Your worth doesn't depend on applause—it's found in those small, courageous, and authentic actions you take every single day.

In our exploration of human desires, we saw how many of us long for belonging, connection, and validation. Yet we discovered that real belonging doesn't come from fitting in or meeting others' expectations. It's about being seen and loved for who you truly are. When you align with your values and beliefs, your worth will shine through, unapologetically.

Now, more than ever, it's clear: our worth is not defined by success, wealth, or status. What truly matters is how we show up in the world—living authentically, in alignment with our values. The gifts, abilities, and strengths we possess are the tools to unlock our true worth—not in what we do, but in how we do it.

We've also faced the reality of anxiety, worry, and addiction—the burdens that can make us feel less than, unworthy, or broken. But here's the truth: struggling with anxiety doesn't mean you're broken. It means you're human. You are worthy of compassion, healing, and growth, no matter where you are on your journey.

Change is inevitable, and it often comes with discomfort. But we've seen that the messiness of life's transitions offers us the opportunity to transform. Every time you lean into uncertainty, you build resilience, strengthening your sense of worth. By adapting to change, overcoming hurdles, and embracing the unknown, you grow more capable of handling whatever comes your way.

Parting Words

One of the toughest lessons we learned together is how comparison often steals our peace. That pressure to measure up—to be like others—only diminishes our sense of self. But by now, it should be clear: your worth doesn't come from being anyone other than yourself. It comes from being unapologetically you—the wonderful, unique, amazing you. Stay true to your values, and let that be the only measure of your worth.

Throughout these pages, we've talked a lot about mindfulness, which is the most powerful tool you have in this journey. With distractions constantly pulling you in every direction, it's easy to get lost in the 'achieve or fail' mentality. But by staying present, by carving out time for yourself to just be, you reconnect with your inherent worth. That's where it resides—right in the present moment, free from the noise.

We also explored the importance of building a supportive tribe. No one is meant to go through life alone. Healthy relationships help us feel seen, heard, and valued. Surround yourself with people who lift you up, who nourish your soul. If you value your well-being, you must choose relationships that empower you and help you grow.

And finally, we redefined wealth—not just in terms of money or possessions, but in terms of what truly aligns with your values. This, I hope, resonated with you deeply. True wealth isn't measured by what you have; it's measured by how you use what you have to live a life that reflects your true worth.

I want to leave you with something that I hope you carry with you always. Imagine I'm holding a crisp, clean $50 bill. Now, imagine I crumple it up and throw it on the floor, stomp on it, pick it up again. The bill is wrinkled, dirty, maybe even a little stained. But here's the thing: it's still worth $50.

It's the same with your worth. Life will throw challenges your way—there will be times when you feel crumpled, worn down, or worthless. But just like that $50 bill, no matter what happens, your worth doesn't change. It's not tied to your circumstances, your failures, or how others treat you. No matter how messy life gets, no matter how many mistakes you make, your worth is always there, unshaken, unchanged.

Worthy

So, as you move forward from here, remember this: Your worth is unshakable. You are enough, exactly as you are. Choose to show up for yourself, embrace your worth, and live a life that reflects the truth of who you are.

Because, my friend, you are worthy. Always.

Kasmin

ACKNOWLEDGMENTS

Writing this book has been both a personal and professional purpose fulfilled. These ideas have long informed my work with clients, my advice to friends, associates, family—and even strangers—who've encouraged me to share them both publicly and privately for decades.

This book began with *Passion Parties*: events regularly held with circles of professional women seeking to improve their lives across various domains. It evolved to the next level after an evening spent with Jan Miller of Dupree, Miller & Associates, my brother Waraire, and DeVon Franklin.

For years, I'd see Jan at T.D. Jakes events, and she kept urging me to write. After that fated evening in her Highland Park, Dallas,

TX, living room, Waraire told me, *"Kasmin, you've got several stories inside of you, and who better to share them? It's gonna be balla."*

I wrote the initial two chapters in 2017, then paused until January 2025—five months after the untimely death of my brother Waraire, while wrestling with grief, uncertainty, fibromyalgia, and more.

It was then I realized: I finally had something crystallized, grounded in evidence-based instructional methods I learned from the late Stanford professor Mary Budd Rowe.

Her best-known research revealed that most teachers didn't wait long enough after asking students a question. By increasing wait time from one second to at least three, students showed marked improvement in language and logic.

I see this book as evidence-based instruction which will transform the way you relearn and help master complicated ideas if you'll allow it to penetrate your soul.

I am deeply grateful to Khalfani, whose project management acumen held me accountable from the sidelines, ensuring I completed what I set out to do: the first in a trilogy series on living our best lives.

I also extend appreciation to my editing creative, as well as to the circle of support found in Shaari, Lynnette, God mommy Arvis, Mrs. Pat, Stacey, Carmen, Yolanda W, Loreli, Sabina, Charmaine, Dominique, Connie, John, Miriam my USC guardian angel nurse who's become a dear friend, Dr. Chelsea Stone, Dorenda "Mae," Texas Grant, Charvus, Mrs. Glendar, Partos, Pastor James, Cindy Herron-Braggs, Mia–my sister from another mother–thank you for all you've done for Boswell and me, Marlena Webb, my beloved Bel Air Study Circle, and my 'Cali NOLA-8' posse.

Acknowledgments

And to Deon Cole: in the moments I wanted to cry, thank you for resetting my compass with those crack-up belly laughs. You're truly funny, conscious, and *'bout it*. No one gets to say otherwise. The world needs you and your comedy. Pure alchemy.

ABOUT THE AUTHOR

Dr. Kasmin Boswell, a Southern California native, is an Associate Director/Senior Medical Liaison with almost two decades of experience in numerous disciplines— women's health, genetics, dermatology, CNS, nephrology, endocrinology, immunology, migraine, neurology, oncology and oncological palliative care.

Kasmin has secured study funding from leading institutions such as the NIH, CDC, Kaiser Foundation, VAMC, Queens Hospital, Stanford, UCSF, UCLA, Rady, Harvard, and RAND.

Throughout her career, she has helped former employers obtain Medicare & Medicaid formulary approval as well as Tier 1 coverage with Blue Cross, Health Net and several divisions within Kaiser Foundation, Swedish, HCA Healthcare, Cleveland Clinic Network, Universal Health Services, Tenet Healthcare, Community Health Systems, Veterans Administration for personalized genomic testing developed by Mayo Clinic. She also regularly leverages her strong relationships within academic and medical centers of excellence to acquire FDA/EUA approvals.

Kasmin's mission is to develop professional relationships with thought leaders, facilitate study recruitment and business development opportunities, and IIR/IST research opportunities. She also provides timely, next generation product information to both internal and external stakeholders.

In addition to her work within the pharmaceutical sector, Kasmin supports individuals entering the pharmaceutical and related industries, helps establish disease advocacy groups for patients and caregivers, and assists patients in gaining access to medications through favorable prior authorization outcomes.

Outside of healthcare, Kasmin has co-owned a clothing business with her brother, Waraire Boswell, since 2003. They design uniforms for McDonald's, ready-to-wear collections, custom pieces, and collaborations for high-profile clients in the entertainment industry.

In her free time, she's passionate about attending estate sales, enjoying great martinis, and volunteering.

REFERENCES AND CITATIONS

1. Bailey, C. (2018). Hyperfocus: How to be more productive in a world of distraction. Penguin US.
2. Baumeister, R. F., Bratslavsky, E., Muraven, M., & Tice, D. M. (1998). Ego depletion: Is the active self a limited resource? Journal of Personality and Social Psychology, 74(5), 1252–1265. https://doi.org/10.1037/0022-3514.74.5.1252
3. Beck, A. T. (2011). Cognitive therapy: Basics and beyond (2nd ed.). The Guilford Press.
4. Borkovec, T. D. (1998). Generalized anxiety disorder: A review of the literature. Journal of Clinical Psychology, 54(5), 557–572. https://pubmed.ncbi.nlm.nih.gov/23537486/
5. Brach, T. (2003). Radical acceptance. Rider & Co.
6. Brickman, P. D., & Campbell, D. T. (1971). Hedonic relativism and planning the good society. In M. H. Appley (Ed.), Adaptation-level theory. Academic Press.
7. Brooks, D. (2015). The road to character. Random House Trade Paperbacks.
8. Brown, B. (2010). The gifts of imperfection. Hazelden Publishing.
9. Brown, B. (2015). Daring greatly: How the courage to be vulnerable transforms the way we live, love, parent, and lead. Penguin Life.

10. Burkeman, O. (2021). Four thousand weeks: Time management for mortals. Farrar, Straus and Giroux.
11. Cacioppo, J. T., & Patrick, W. (2008). Loneliness: Human nature and the need for social connection. W. W. Norton & Co.
12. Covey, S. (1989). The 7 habits of highly effective people. Simon & Schuster.
13. Centers for Disease Control and Prevention. (2023, August 10). Provisional suicide deaths in the United States, 2022. https://www.cdc.gov/media/releases/2023/s0810-US-Suicide-Deaths-2022.html
14. Davidson, R. J., & Begley, S. (2012). The emotional life of your brain: How its unique patterns affect the way you think, feel, and live—and how you can change them. Hudson Street Press.
15. Deci, E. L., & Ryan, R. M. (2000). Self-determination theory and the facilitation of intrinsic motivation, social development, and well-being. American Psychologist, 55(1), 68–78. https://doi.org/10.1037/0003-066X.55.1.68
16. Diamandis, P. H. (2012). Abundance: The future is better than you think. Free Press.
17. Dickinson, E. I Dwell in Possibility. Fascicle 22, circa 1862. Houghton Library, Harvard University.
18. Doidge, N. (2007). The brain that changes itself: Stories of personal triumph from the frontiers of brain science. Viking.
19. Duckworth, A. (2016). Grit: The power of passion and perseverance. Scribner.
20. Eisenberger, N. I. (2012). Broken hearts and broken bones: A neural perspective on the similarities between social and physical pain. Current Directions in Psychological Science, 21(1), 42–47. https://doi.org/10.1177/0963721411429455
21. Eisenberger, N. I. (2012). The pain of social disconnection: Examining the shared neural underpinnings of physical and social pain. Nature Reviews Neuroscience, 13(6), 421–434. https://doi.org/10.1038/nrn3231

References and Citations

22. Emmons, R. A., & McCullough, M. E. (2003). Counting blessings versus burdens: An experimental investigation of gratitude and subjective well-being in daily life. Journal of Personality and Social Psychology, 84(2), 377–389. https://doi.org/10.1037/0022-3514.84.2.377
23. Emmons, R. A., McCullough, M. E., & Tsang, J.-A. (2003). The assessment of gratitude. In S. J. Lopez & C. R. Snyder (Eds.), Positive psychological assessment: A handbook of models and measures (pp. 327–341). American Psychological Association. https://doi.org/10.1037/10612-021
24. Feiler, B. (2020). Life is in the transitions: Mastering change at any age. Penguin Press.
25. Fardouly, J., Diedrichs, P. C., Vartanian, L. R., & Halliwell, E. (2015). Social comparisons on social media: The impact of Facebook on young women's body image concerns and mood. Body Image, 13(1), 29–35. https://doi.org/10.1016/j.bodyim.2014.12.002
26. Frankl, V. E. (2006). Man's search for meaning (Kindle ed.). Beacon Press.
27. Franco, M. G. (2022). Platonic: How the science of attachment can help you make—and keep—friends. Bluebird.
28. Gilbert, P. (2009). The compassionate mind: A new approach to life's challenges. New Harbinger Publications.
29. Grant, A. (2013). Give and take: Why helping others drives our success. Penguin Books.
30. Grant, A., & Sandberg, S. (2017). Option B: Facing adversity, building resilience, and finding joy. Alfred A. Knopf.
31. Haidt, J. (2006). The happiness hypothesis: Finding modern truth in ancient wisdom. William Heinemann Ltd.
32. Harris, T. (2019, December 11). The problem isn't addiction—it's hijacked attention. Center for Humane Technology. https://www.humanetech.com/problem

33. Hoge, E. A., Bui, E., Palitz, S. A., Schwarz, N. R., Owens, M. E., & Wetherell, J. L. (2013). The effect of mindfulness meditation on anxiety and depression: A meta-analytic review. Journal of Consulting and Clinical Psychology, 81(1), 168–178. https://doi.org/10.1037/a0033005
34. Holt-Lunstad, J., Smith, T. B., Baker, M., Harris, T., & Stephenson, D. (2015). Loneliness and social isolation as risk factors for mortality: A meta-analytic review. Perspectives on Psychological Science, 10(2), 227–237. https://doi.org/10.1177/1745691614568352
35. Holiday, R. (2014). The obstacle is the way: The timeless art of turning trials into triumph. Portfolio.
36. Jellinger, K. A. (2023). Depression in dementia with Lewy bodies: A critical update. Journal of Neural Transmission, 130(5), 247–257. https://doi.org/10.1007/s00702-023-02669-8
37. Jetten, J., Haslam, C., & Haslam, S. (2012). The social cure: Identity health and wellbeing. Psychology Press.
38. Kahneman, D., & Deaton, A. (2010). High income improves evaluation of life but not emotional well-being. Proceedings of the National Academy of Sciences of the U.S.A., 107(38), 16489–16493. https://doi.org/10.1073/pnas.1011492107
39. Kasser, T., & Ryan, R. M. (1996). Further examining the American dream: Differential correlates of intrinsic and extrinsic goals. Personality and Social Psychology Bulletin, 22(3), 280–287. https://doi.org/10.1177/0146167296223006
40. Kishimi, I., & Koga, F. (2018). The courage to be disliked. Allen & Unwin.
41. Klontz, B., & Klontz, T. (2009). Mind over money: Overcoming the money disorders that threaten our financial health. Crown Business.
42. Lao Tzu. (2022). Tao te ching. Simon & Brown.
43. Lacy, S. (2018). Jane Fonda in 5 Acts [Film]. HBO.

References and Citations

44. Leaf, C. (2021). Cleaning up your mental mess: 5 simple, scientifically proven steps to reduce anxiety, stress, and toxic thinking. Baker Books.
45. Maté, G. (2008). In the realm of hungry ghosts: Close encounters with addiction. North Atlantic Books.
46. Neff, K. (2015). Self-compassion: The proven power of being kind to yourself. William Morrow Paperbacks.
47. Newport, C. (2016). Deep work. Piatkus.
48. O'Hara, D. (2017, December 18). The intrinsic motivation of Richard Ryan and Edward Deci. American Psychological Association. https://www.apa.org/members/content/intrinsic-motivation
49. Palihapitiya, C. (2017, December 11). Quoted in Wong, J. C. Former Facebook executive: Social media is ripping society apart. The Guardian. https://www.theguardian.com/technology/2017/dec/11/facebook-former-executive-ripping-society-apart
50. Toller, E. (2014). The power of now: A guide to spiritual enlightenment. New World Library.
51. Pink, D. H. (2011). Drive: The surprising truth about what motivates us. Riverhead Books.
52. Ressler, K. J., & Mayberg, H. S. (2018). Targeting abnormal neural circuits in mood and anxiety disorders: From the laboratory to the clinic. Nature Neuroscience, 21(11), 1375–1385. https://doi.org/10.1038/s41593-018-0245-0
53. Robin, V., & Dominguez, J. (2018). Your money or your life: 9 steps to transforming your relationship with money and achieving financial independence. Penguin Books.
54. Ryan, R. M., & Deci, E. L. (2000). Self-determination theory and the facilitation of intrinsic motivation, social development, and well-being. American Psychologist, 55(1), 68–78. https://doi.org/10.1037/0003-066X.55.1.68

55. Schwartz, B. (2004). The paradox of choice: Why more is less. Harper Perennial.
56. Seligman, M. E. P. (2011). Flourish: A visionary new understanding of happiness and well-being. Atria Books.
57. Strayed, C. (2012). Wild: From lost to found on the Pacific Crest Trail. Alfred A. Knopf.
58. Sutherland, D. (2014). The art of stillness: Adventures in going nowhere. Penguin.
59. Tiggemann, M., & Slater, M. (2013). NetGirls: The Internet, Facebook, and body image concern in adolescent girls. International Journal of Eating Disorders, 46(6), 630–633. https://doi.org/10.1002/eat.23023
60. Twist, L., & Barker, T. (2003). The soul of money: Transforming your relationship with money and life. W. W. Norton & Company.
61. Vallerand, R. J., & Houlfort, N. (2018). The role of passion in sustainable fulfillment. Springer.
62. Young, J. (2016). The inner game of tennis: The classic guide to the mental side of peak performance. Vintage.

www.ingramcontent.com/pod-product-compliance
Lightning Source LLC
Chambersburg PA
CBHW030451100526
44580CB00005B/82/J